BON

The L. Ron Hubbard Series

BRIDGE PUBLICATIONS, INC.
5600 E. Olympic Blvd.
Commerce, California 90022 USA

ISBN 978-1-4031-9878-5

Special acknowledgment is made to the L. Ron Hubbard Library for permission to reproduce photographs from his personal collection. Additional credits: pp. 4 & 5, 6 Andreas Feininger/Time & Life Pictures/Getty Images; pp. 10 & 11 Tatiana53/Shutterstock.com; pp. 12 & 13 American Stock Photography, Inc.; p. 15 National Archives; p. 18 Security Pacific National Bank Collection/Los Angeles Public Library; p. 20 Jim Daly Photography Studio; p. 23 Amy Toensing/Getty Images; p. 34 New York Public Library; pp. 48, 91 © Earl Theisen/Roxann Livingston; p. 49 Gene Lester/Getty Images; p. 55 Library of Congress, Prints & Photographs Division, LC-DIG-ggbain-01672; p. 58 Gene Lester/Hulton Archive/Getty Images; pp. 66 & 67 Frescomovie/Shutterstock.com; p. 69 Alexkar08/Shutterstock.com; p. 70 Los Angeles Public Library; p. 78 Yory Frenklakh/Shutterstock.com; pp. 84 & 85 R-studio/Shutterstock.com; p. 89 University of California Los Angeles; pp. 92, 93 Missouri Valley Special Collections, Kansas City Public Library, Kansas City, Missouri; pp. 94 & 95 Archive Photo/Getty Images; p. 105 Getty Images; pp. 110 & 111 Fox Photos/Getty Images; pp. 118 & 119 Peter Stackpole/Getty Images.

Editor Letter p. 35; illustration, Editor Letter & Letters to Editor pp. 37–40; illustration p. 42; illustration p. 43: *Astounding Science Fiction* copyright © by Street & Smith Publications, Inc. Reprinted with permission of Penny Publications, LLC.

John W. Campbell, Jr., letter of December 23, 1949, appearing on pp. 24 & 25 reproduced with permission of AC Projects, Inc.

Robert A. Heinlein letter of April 17, 1950, appearing on p. 53 courtesy of University of California, Santa Cruz.

Printed in the United States of America

The L. Ron Hubbard Series: Dianetics Letters & Journals—English

The L. Ron Hubbard Series

DIANETICS
LETTERS &
JOURNALS

Bridge

PUBLICATIONS, INC.®

CONTENTS

By JOHN CLARKE
(Daily News Staff Writer)

L. Ron Hubbard is a sometime engineer, mathematician, philosopher, naval officer and prolific producer of science fiction of the space ship, or fantastic school of literature.

He is, more, by his own account, an independent thinker and as such a rebel against Authority and Orthodoxy.

(Continued from page 2)

was obvious that mind meters body function." He was later to conclude that "what has been called mind is really in two sections: first, there is the endocrine system which, handled either by the analytical mind ... or the reactive mind ... brings emotional responses of fear, enthusiasm, apathy, etc." Glands were an instrument of body control!

Hubbard confesses he finally tired of listening with half an ear to lectures repeating the dictums of authority while he was doing his own thinking on other planes, and he left the university sans degree.

He went on...

solely as a pulp author.
potboilers was a living
to an end. He regarded
and always the scholar.

By 1935 he was rea...
some of the basic resea...
1938 the primary axiom...
had been discovered an...
Hubbard at that time w...
tempted to send up a tri...
that he wrote a book e...
the principles of his sc...
he allowed the book t...
unpublished.

"I knew what the p...
but I did not know...

TATE OF MISSOURI
C HOSPITAL, NO. 3
NEVADA, MISSOURI

SAMUEL MARSH
DIRECTOR
PUBLIC HEALTH AND WELFARE

B. E. RAGLAND
DIRECTOR
DIVISION OF MENTAL DISEASES

20 July 1950

sh Foundation Inc.

d two more names to the list of those who
d the institute for training in Dianetics?
to be considered when training is started.

et clear, nor for that matter do we have
lade progress with each other. I have
one patient and have made progress with
e I am doing little else.)

F. Lamoreaux,R.N.,knows a good deal of
ough she tended to fight with it before,
She lacks but a years residence for her

Dear Friend:

L. Ron Hubbard will make...
Los Angeles at a Dianetic meet...
Auditorium, Thursday at 8 P.M...
is president of the Hubbard Di...

Foundation schedule course...
direction of Mr. Hubbard on Au...

An Associate Membership in...
individuals interested in Dianet...
receives, through the bulletin l...
of new developments in Dianetics...
house for Dianetic data. The mem...
annually.

Discussion groups and Dianet...
lished in the Los Angeles area. T...
for a splendid piece of pioneerin...

With Dianetics as a swiftly...
discoveries and improved techniqu...
methods that have been verified b...
These will be demonstrated at the...
The Los Angeles Department is like...
emphasize Research as well as tra...

Sloane 4972

Dear Mr. Hubbard,

I know every minute of your...
had to write – propitiation or no...
I think you have given to the wo...
whether postulated or not, as fe...
reading your book DIANETICS was...
perplexities, resolved for me fo...
mind, but one who was eager to...
it happened to me when I was al...
with the inadequacy of words, a...
always known that I know', you...
interpret my sincere thank you...
needed you, and will one day ae...
can!

After DIANETICS, I joined...
stout body of some 50 to 80 pe...
crowded island! – and our aim...
process the numbers we know w...
on. And that is a source of...
so few, and those few are not...
simplest cases. I studied ev...
wholeheartedly that "the pre...
etc.etc." Yes, auditors alt...
important, and there is no o...
mind, my reactive mind that...
my straight memory is indee...
determined on such a life a...
from birth up, few could w...

That being so, I went...
and Self Analysis, but I fi...
my mind, that somehow, in a...
difficulties. I...

ily News

DEPENDENT NEWSPAPER FOR INDEPENDENT PEOPLE

king U.S. by storm

a pulp author. Hacki...
rs was a living and a...
d. He regarded himse...
ays the scholar and su...
935 he was ready to...
the basic research, an...
e primary axioms of...
n discovered and for...
d at that time was so...
d to send up a trial bu...
wrote a book embra...
nciples of his science...
wed the book to lan...
ished.

knew what the princ...
lid not know if they...
" he now freely adm...
was not until 12 yea...
ntains of research late...
decided he did know...
e a book meant for...

RESEARCH FOUNDATION
024, L.A.5
7-3194

July 26, 1950

his first public appearance in...
ing to be held in the Shrine...
, August 10, 1950. Mr. Hubbard...
ianetic Research Foundation.

ses will open under the personal...
August 14, 1950.

in the Foundation is open to...
anetics. An Associate Member...
n issued periodically. informatio...
tics, which will act as a clearing...
membership is fifteen dollars...

Dianetic clubs already are estab-...
rea. They are to be congratulated...
oneering work.

wiftly advancing science, new...

At last — A True Science of the Mind

DIANETICS

The Modern Science of Mental Health
A HANDBOOK OF MODERN THERAPY

By L. RON HUBBARD

This book reveals the results of fifteen years of study and research on the working of the human mind. Tackling the problem by the scientific method, the author has discovered what he believes to be the source of all mental and psychosomatic ills, and has developed a technique of Dianetic Therapy that has worked successfully for every one of the two hundred and seventy unselected cases treated and tested.

Dianetics offers this totally new therapeutic technique with which physicians, psychiatrists, psychoanalysts, and others, can treat inorganic mental and organic psychosomatic ills. Sufficient details are presented so that any experimenter can duplicate and check the validity of the theories and postulates of Dianetics.

The author and his associates invite the testing by modern medical and scientific workers, using standard scientific methods, of any one and all of the claims made in this book. *Dianetics* also contains circuit graphs by Donald H. Rogers, an evaluation of philosophic method by Will Durant, and a statement of scientific method by John W. Campbell, nuclear physicist and author of *The Atomic Story*. $4.00

PSYCHOANALYSIS:
EVOLUTION AND DEVELOPMENT
A Review of Theory and Therapy
By CLARA THOMPSON, M.D.
With the collaboration of PATRICK MULLAHY

Use coupon to order your books today.

"I strongly recommend Psychoanalysis: Evolution and Development by Clara Thompson to all readers of A S F. It is a clear, definite and interesting account of the problems and developments of psychoanalysis."

Angeles Times SUNDAY, J...

BEST SE...

OS ANGELES
es records of Broadway,
Campbell's, Fowler
y Co. and Robinson's.)

An Introductory Note

From the greater treasury of L. Ron Hubbard Archives comes a highly illuminating collection of personal letters and autobiographical journals. All told, these materials span the whole of L. Ron Hubbard's life—from his first extraordinary steps of adventure and discovery to his ultimate triumph with the founding of Dianetics and Scientology. Accordingly (and albeit representing but a fraction of his archival material), these papers provide exquisite depth and color to a most extraordinary life. Hence, this special, supplemental edition within the larger L. Ron Hubbard Series: L. Ron Hubbard's Letters & Journals.

The Dianetics Letters:
An Introduction

"I T ALL BEGAN," EXPLAINED L. RON HUBBARD, "WHEN I FIRST released twelve years of independent research into the field of the mind." What followed is, of course, all we now know as the revelation of Dianetics and all that subject represents as a global force for the betterment of Man. But if the general history of that movement has

been told—how L. Ron Hubbard came to unleash *Dianetics: The Modern Science of Mental Health,* how that book took America by storm through the summer of 1950 and subsequently became the most popular self-help text in publishing history—then here is the history from the eye of that storm. That is, here is the correspondence of L. Ron Hubbard from the advent of a discovery that forever changed our conception of who we are and what we are capable of as human beings.

The letters herein span six crucial years between the development of Dianetics as a workable method for self-discovery to the utilization of that method across three continents. Although not absolutely necessary for an appreciation of what we present in the pages to follow, let us supply a few words on the subject proper. In the first place, let us

describe Dianetics as an actual *technology* of the mind, a method of plumbing that "vast and hitherto unknown realm half an inch back of our foreheads." In the second place, let us understand Dianetics is a wholly precise practice and in no way similar to the aimless introspection of Gestalten schools or the haphazard rambling of the psychoanalyst. On the contrary, Dianetics auditing is a most exact "tracing of experience" to relieve the source of all psychosomatic ills and aberrant behavior. Or as Ron himself defines it: "Dianetics is the route from aberrated (or aberrated and ill) human to capable human." Finally, let us understand that Dianetics works, and the miracles referenced through the pages of these letters are both real and routine, as in: "A little girl bedridden for twelve years is now walking after only five hours of auditing."

"It all began when I first released twelve years of independent research…" —LRH, Elizabeth, New Jersey, 1950

Dianetics

The greek letter Delta is the basic form. Green for growth, yellow for life.

The four stripes represent the four dynamics of Dianetics, Survival as I self, II sex and family, III group and IV Mankind.

This symbol was designed and used since 1950.

Yet the real subject of these letters is neither Dianetics as a technology for miracles nor the worldwide movement those miracles finally inspired. Rather, the subject here is L. Ron Hubbard himself—from his first bold step into that once forbidden netherworld of human thought to the honing of methods, techniques and nomenclature ("an outgrowth of redefinition of the character of the mind and an examination of the exact causation and effectiveness of traumas"). Here, too, is a first formally published explanation of Dianetics appearing in *The Explorers Journal*—aptly titled *Terra Incognita: The Mind* and providing all basic Dianetics theory. (While in reply, here is the Club's redefinition of exploration to include that step into a vast unknown behind the human forehead.) Then again, here is

L. Ron Hubbard in the New Jersey birthplace of *Dianetics* where "the ocean is just outside the front door but it knows its place and never makes a real nuisance of itself," and yet again at the site of the first public lectures where he found himself obliged to inform the landlord: "Happily for me if unhappily for you I have a book on the bestseller lists. The volume of traffic cannot be stopped."

Additionally germane to this story are those letters pertaining to the equally extraordinary backlash from a covetous psychiatric establishment and what ensued from that onslaught in Wichita, Kansas, circa 1952. Then, too, here he is with colleagues, associates and such longtime friends as the science fiction master Robert Heinlein. Also included is a wonderfully irascible author, inventor and occasional farmer by the name of Russell Hays. And if the private L. Ron Hubbard of these letters is finally the same as the public L. Ron Hubbard, then here he is even more so: "I am not god or an angel. I'm just another guy. But I'm a guy with a job to do and a guy who, amongst all these, is peculiarly fitted to do that job."

To Ron's earliest references regarding "this research on the mind," we further include his formal statement to psychological circles

and several less formal notes from the first Dianetic Research Foundations. Also included are selections from the storm of replies to the publication of Book One and correspondence from the birthplace of that work at Bay Head, New Jersey. Then again we offer a most significant LRH challenge to psychiatric circles—a challenge for results no psychiatrist would accept.

But remembering this story is ultimately one of discovery and triumph, let us introduce these letters as LRH himself introduced this subject more than half a century ago: "You are beginning an adventure. Treat it as an adventure. And may you never be the same again." ∎

CHAPTER ONE

Letter from a
LONGSHOREMAN

Letter from a
Longshoreman

AMONG THE MORE THAN THREE HUNDRED SUBJECTS receiving early Dianetics processing through the course of LRH research prior to the publication of *Dianetics* was a particularly ailing New York longshoreman by the name of Dennis Rittwager. If the story is a famous one—Ron himself remarks upon the case in later lectures—the

critical letter only recently surfaced amidst stacks of correspondence from the spring of 1950. To Ron's on-the-scene report and the very self-explanatory longshoreman letter itself, we might further paint the scene as follows:

Having entered Manhattan some weeks earlier, Ron had made his way to the Hell's Kitchen loft of celebrated portraitist Hubert "Matty" Mathieu ("a dear friend, stamped with youth on the Left Bank of the Seine and painting dowagers at the Beaux-Arts in middle age," as LRH explains in his own highly celebrated *ART*). There, a fairly traditional Thanksgiving dinner commenced with iced sherry as a prelude to turkey. For the less prosperously neighboring Rittwagers, however, that Thanksgiving eve, 1946, held a very different fare.

By way of two ancillary notes: Although injections of penicillin (then readily available over-the-counter) are generally sufficient to halt the spread of gangrenous infection, seriously affected tissue typically requires amputation. It becomes even more significant, then, that Rittwager lost not even a toe after the employment of Dianetics to relieve emotionally encysted grief, i.e., "He cried as he told me how he'd bought a little farm...." ∎

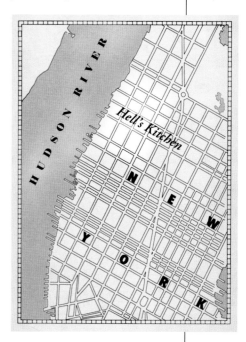

Left New York longshoremen, circa 1945

26 Nov

I came a bit too soon but week-ended with Matty then moved into a nice room—at this hotel—Sunday night. But Monday spent with John Campbell—stayed there all night. Still having this room. Then this evening with Matty.

Matty wants me to write a column he will illustrate. One of these maybe schemes. Then there is a new magazine somebody wants and Matty and I have a conference on that tomorrow at 4 with some people. I have been asked to lay out their format and editorial policy. Then Matty has a school for arts in project but I am not much interested though the people want me to teach the writing. Too indefinite an idea—too mundane.

Had an adventure tonight. Mat went next door and here lay a man nearly dead of an infected foot. The foot was swollen double size and black, a fireball in the groin, red streaks and high fever. I started out to get him sulfa but bought penicillin instead. 33,000 unit shots. This was about six, first shot at seven. I taught his wife to shoot him, and then went back to supervise the 10:00 PM and 01:00 AM shots. His fever broke before 1:00 but I am still wondering if he will save that foot. The whole place smells sweet with gangrene. He was both poor and foolish. Squalor such as his surrounding are tenement usuals in the East. Five children, a wife harassed by filth and malnutrition. Children eating filth from gutters. Uneducated, unventilated quarters. Illness interrupting jobs. And they had planned a lovely Christmas for he was working for a change. And then Saturday a clinic which called blood poisoning "Athlete's Foot" and there amid tangled, filthy quilts in a dingy, dirty room where hungry and half sick kids cry, a man lies dying, an ugly little man, beaten by Catholicism, Capitalism, ignorance. And he cried as he told me how he'd bought a little farm for 800 dollars and how he wanted his wife, who disliked town, to be happy there. A man who had starved and slaved to forty-three and now had nothing.

At 1:00 his foot looked even blacker but the fever had broken. I did not trust any doctor or hospital: I know New York. Tomorrow, I pray, he may be well. A miracle will have happened.

Ron

August 12
1950

My Dear Doc,

Just a line to Express my thanks to you, also to let you know that I have not forgotten what you did by Saving my Life. If you did not happen to be in the neighborhood at the time I would not be here today to say God Bless you and that you achieve what you set out to do for mankind. And may God give you a long Life in which to achieve the things you Plan. Doc from the bottom of my Heart

again I say God Bless you and
Thanks a Million.
Doc, they were all ready to cut
the leg off, but it is Fine Now.
Thanks to you that is all
I can say.
        I remain respectfully yours
the Man who's Life you saved
in Hells Kitchen 3 Years ago.

                    Dennis P. Kittwagles
                    4/33 West 48. St.
                    New York City

The Jersey Shore, circa 1950

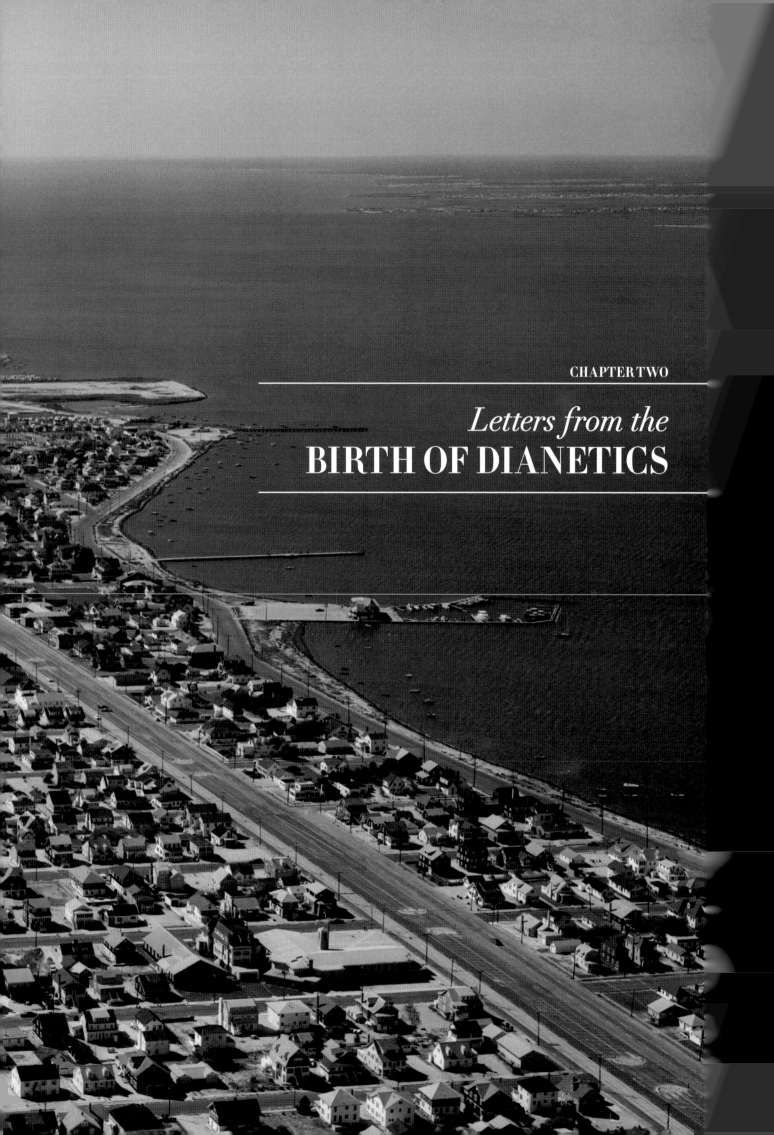

CHAPTER TWO

Letters from the
BIRTH OF DIANETICS

Letters from the

Birth of Dianetics

THOSE FAMILIAR WITH THE LIFE OF L. RON HUBBARD AS recounted in this series will recall repeated references to the LRH trail of research through the latter 1940s. Generally touched upon are his 1945 endocrinological studies at an Oak Knoll Naval Hospital in Oakland, his 1946 examination of narcosynthesis at a California Veterans Administration, his 1947 work with neurotics from the Hollywood film community and his 1948 treatment of the criminally insane in a Savannah, Georgia, institution. Also routinely mentioned is Ron's first formal description of results in a widely circulated *Original Thesis,* his presentation of discoveries to an American medical and psychiatric establishment, his rebuff from that establishment and, finally, his authoring of a broadly accessible Dianetics Handbook in a beachfront home in New Jersey. Never previously offered, however, is what appears here: the actual correspondence from which we draw so much of the color and detail found in the *L. Ron Hubbard Series.*

For example: from the literal road of discovery LRH traveled through these years comes his most revealing letter to Russell Hays. An author, inventor and gentleman farmer, Hays had counted himself among Ron's closest friends for more than two decades. Both shared an abiding fascination with primitive cultures, aeronautics and that *Terra Incognita* of the human mind—the subject of Ron's letter here.

Below
Oak Knoll
Naval Hospital,
Oakland,
California

Left The author of Dianetics renown, spring 1950

Letters from the Birth of Dianetics 15

Below
The Bay
Head, New
Jersey, beach
house where
L. Ron Hubbard
authored
*Dianetics: The
Modern Science
of Mental Health*

Quite in addition to above-mentioned LRH letters to the American Medical and Psychiatric Associations, we offer Ron's summary description of Dianetics to the Gerontological Society in Baltimore, Maryland. Of particular interest—and found nowhere else—is Ron's reference to that Oak Knoll experimentation wherein former prisoners of war responded to hormonal therapy only after "the removal of the early traumas" through Dianetic procedures.

Although much has been said regarding author-editor John W. Campbell, Jr.'s publication of Ron's *Evolution of a Science* in *Astounding Science Fiction,* here is what Campbell himself had to say on the matter. Here, too, is J. W. Campbell, Jr., on the forthcoming *Dianetics: The Modern Science of Mental Health* and what he rightly foresaw as the backlash from a deeply flawed psychiatric community.

Finally, and for a rare LRH description of the actual *Dianetics* birthplace, comes a second telling note to Russell Hays from the "wilds" of Bay Head, New Jersey. ∎

General Delivery
El Cajon, Calif.

July 15, 1948

Dear Russell;

Went through our old home town t'other day and you'd sure have to look hard to see much change. Drug stores, theater, p.o., your place, bums on the beach and all seem to be complete to the smallest detail. Was going to stop there but somehow rolled on by it and couldn't find my brakes until El Cajon.

Been amusing myself making a monkey out of Freud. I always knew he was nutty but didn't have a firm case. Recall that book* that knocked me off my hinges about ten years back? Well, I sensibly kept it in mothballs as too hot to handle. A publisher offered to publish it couple months back and I broke it out and then shook my head over it. So instead I took a little section of one chapter and began to work on it and all of a sudden it seemed like I'd been awful dumb ten years back about the hooman mind—if any—because I'd overlooked the lengths one could go in that department. Then I started on "inferiority complexes" and nightly had people writhing in my Hollywood office, sending guys out twice as tall as superman. The most satisfactory work of all was on allergies and stuttering and these were scotched in two or three hours per case. In short, although I won't bank on it until I get a complete stress analysis, on this here bridge, I seem to have cut psycho-analysis down from a two year job to about two nights. Here and there I hit a mental hypochondriac who is so much in love with his mental ill health that he just plain can't live without it. I'm working on that now.

The indomitable Russell Hays

*In reference to the 120,000-word "Excalibur," authored in 1938 and comprising a first philosophic plateau toward the founding of Dianetics.

This is an outgrowth of re-definition of the character of the mind and an examination of the exact causation and effectiveness of traumas.

A psychiatrist, who can do practically nothing for anybody; he uses psycho-analysis; he works two to three years on a customer—you can't say patient because nothing much is being done for him but you will admit that besides being a fool he *is* patient—at the rate of four visits per week of one hour each at a cost of $15 per visit and after an $8,000 expenditure ordinarily manages a few minor aberrations or maybe an allergy and discharges his customer for future reference. Well, I've been rolling this sort of thing back to twenty hours of work average for a total cure and complete shift of personality. Takes as high as fifty hours of work sometimes, but the thing works on about 80% of all patients, sane or otherwise.

My very best—
Ron

El Cajon, California

Box 1796
Savannah, Ga.

April 13, 1949

The Gerontological Soc.,
Baltimore City Hospital,
Baltimore, Md.

Gentlemen;

Working in private research, I have apparently made certain discoveries which seem to indicate they would have a definite effect on longevity. As a society member I am communicating a brief outline.

I am accumulating additional information to safeguard this work from undue optimism and am preparing a paper, a copy of which will be sent to you, entitled, Certain Discoveries and Researches Leading to the Removal of Early Traumatic Experiences Including Attempted Abortion, Birth Shock and Infant Illnesses and Accidents with an Examination of their Effects Physiological and Psychological and their Potential Influence on Longevity on the Adult Individual with an Account of the Techniques Evolved and Employed.

A very brief résumé of this work follows: In an effort to evolve a better clinical approach to the treatment of certain neuroses and psychoses, to permanently relieve psycho-somatic ills and to investigate some of the longevity factors, an extensive investigation of the early work of Freud was undertaken and revealed certain premises. First amongst these was the belief that the unconscious mind recalled birth shock. Lack of technology made it impossible for Freud to pursue that work at that time. By making changes in the practices of narco-synthesis and combining it with certain techniques of hypnosis but employing no positive suggestion or other therapy peculiar to hypnosis, a trance state was induced in patients and, with these evolved techniques, they were induced to recall the birth trauma. A series of twenty cases was examined. Eight of the first ten recalled birth. New significance was found in traumatic experience and a method was evolved to remove early traumas completely. During therapy on the next ten cases, in four subjects earlier traumatic experience was found to precede birth such as accident to the mother and attempted abortion and these traumas were removed in order to reach and relieve the birth shock. In each case treated the removal of the early traumas brought about a marked improvement in the psychological and physiological health of the adult, a removal of psychoses and psycho-somatic illnesses such as arthritis, sinusitis, allergies, asthma, peptic ulcers and chronic headaches including one migraine, the only patient so suffering.

One decided aspect, present in sixteen of the cases out of twenty, was the reduction of the physiological age of the adult, clinically measurable by exercise tests. Another aspect was the apparent new effectiveness of hormones which, in hormone-therapy prior to this treatment, had not been effective and which, after the removal of the early traumas and a subsequent removal of other serious traumatic experiences, were not found to be as vital to the individual if more effective. A third longevity aspect was the improvement of four of these cases suffering from heart trouble which would now seem to have been psycho-somatic although other causes had been assigned: the lunge of the heart at the cutting of the umbilical cord had been restimulated steadily by present environment until the heart was in poor condition.

In one case of arrested sexual development, a girl and the only one present in this series of twenty, the glands renewed activity without hormone-therapy and she underwent a physiological change toward normal.

This letter may be considered only as a report of work-in-progress as an additional twenty cases are to be studied before any final conclusion is drawn and then, of course, it can only be tentative, awaiting the experience of other investigators advised by my discoveries. A paper as mentioned above will be released at the end of the next series.

Saint Joseph's Hospital, Savannah, Georgia

You have permission, however, to publish this letter providing this injunction is added: there is no particular danger involved in working in this field except when the early traumas are approached and restimulated but not removed by therapy. In such an untoward event one sees the history of physiological and psychological deterioration markedly accelerated since it seems possible from these studies that such deterioration is caused by present environment gradually causing the unconscious integration of the early traumas with their force and psychotic or neurotic significance: once the environment restimulates the early traumatic experience that experience apparently remains restimulated. Hence restimulation of an early trauma by therapy but not its removal occasions deterioration of the individual to greater or lesser degree. However my final conclusions are reserved until, at least, the end of the next series.

Sincerely,
L. Ron Hubbard

Bay Head, New Jersey

Nov. 14, 1949

Dear Russell,

Thank you so much for the skunk cabbage. It was just what I wanted. Nothing could have been sweeter. However, your letter left much to be desired. If you had nothing better to say you shouldn't have said anything at all.

I am dug down here in a very nice wind break. I have eight bedrooms here to wander around and contemplate. If you get tired of the wilds of Kansas you are hereby invited to come down and view the wilds of New Jersey.

The ocean is just outside the front door but it knows its place and never makes a real nuisance of itself. And if it does, why, we just go to a movie until the house has settled back down on its foundations again.

Right now there are a couple of writers staying here. They weren't invited guests like yourself. They just stopped by for dinner one night around the first of October. They are wonderful plot material though.

I'm still doing this research on the mind. The results are going to be published soon and then I'll have time to do a little something on the line of stories. I am working on a movie shooting script but that's about all at the present time.

I wish you'd let go and write me one of your famous letters. I think you must be about three behind me by now. Get at least one out before the drifts lock you in for the winter. I'd like to hear what *you* are calling work these days. I always get a laugh out of that.

Thanks again for the spice.

Sincerely,
Ron

ASTOUNDING
SCIENCE FICTION

Dec. 23, 1949

Dear Bob:

I have been busy—mostly the Dianetics stuff. Incidentally, Hubbard's full-scale article, a 16,000 word job, is appearing in the May ASF, and if it doesn't cause something more than a minor explosion I miss my guess considerably. The thing is a direct, complete statement of the development of the idea, showing what led him to it, and stating his results. Simultaneously, the Hermitage House book publishers are bringing out his book giving details of the techniques used. And the editorial in the magazine, that issue, is along the following lines:

All who disagree are invited to submit articles and letters. The best of such articles and letters will be published.

BUT—the letters and articles in argument *must follow the rules of the Scientific Method.*

With John W. Campbell, Jr., at the Bay Head birthplace of *Dianetics,* April 1950

Now that last is a cruel, cruel thing to do to psychiatrists, etc. The scientific method is firmly rooted on two great points: appeal to authority is not evidence and is of no value whatever. No theory, however well-liked and widely accepted, can stand in the face of one single demonstrable fact. And I might have added the Principle of Parsimony—that the *simplest* theory that explains all observed facts, and does not require non-existent phenomena, is the preferred theory.

However, I suggest that the psychiatrists, in working up their arguments, try substituting the name "Doakes" wherever they tend to put "Freud," "Jung," or "Adler," and see if the argument makes sense. It should; facts, not authorities, are the only argumentative basis under the scientific method.

But it's cruel! Can you imagine a psychiatrist trying to discuss the mind without appeal to authority?

The prefrontal lobotomy—which cuts out a piece of the brain of the "incurable" insane patient—is not intended to cure, which it doesn't, but to render the hopeless case more tractable. But it permanently destroys the brain. No psychiatrist would order such an operation if he did not sincerely believe that the case was something no known psychiatric method could cure now, or in the foreseeable future—that, in other words, the known techniques were completely helpless in the face of the problem. Present psycho-therapeutic techniques have, then, been declared inadequate to handle the assigned problem, and have been so declared by the expert practitioners of those techniques!

Regards,
John

Concerning Terra Incognita

"In new and current work my stress is upon man's potential as an effort to turn his mind from the petty intrigues of nations upon a small and unimportant world."—L. Ron Hubbard, winter 1949, in a prefatory word to The Explorers Journal about to publish Terra Incognita.

It was far more fitting than one might imagine. For even as John W. Campbell, Jr., set the stage to publish L. Ron Hubbard's "complete statement" on the development of Dianetics and even as Ron himself entertained offers to author a fully realized Handbook on the subject, here was Dianetics rightfully finding a home in The Explorers Journal.

To explain: while Captain L. Ron Hubbard had long held a place in that league of adventurous gentlemen and long distinguished himself at the helm of expeditions through distant seas and across untrammeled shores, only now was it evident that his exploits in the field and his trail to Dianetics were always, in fact, one and the same. A quarter of a million miles before the age of nineteen, twice to Asia where he drank deep from dread mysteries, twice again to the Caribbean where he searched out a people who were ancient when Columbus arrived—all this and more comprised his path of investigation and what he so modestly describes as the "countless odds and ends" that finally figured into the discovery of Dianetics.

So, yes, the wilderness through which Ron ventured in the name of exploration was the same far country through which he hacked a path to Dianetics. And, yes, appropriately predating both Dianetics: The Evolution of a Science and the Handbook itself was Ron's first formally published explanation of the subject in The Explorers Journal. In consequence, and it was no insignificant matter, just as Dianetics evolved from and for exploration, so the Explorers Club evolved a new perspective on exploration. That is: to not only encourage scientific research of a geographical or ethnological nature, "but research of every kind that takes an individual into the regions of the world, either unknown or but little known, and where contributions to knowledge may be gathered firsthand."

Thus here indeed is exploration of a strange horizon and a dark unknown wherein adventures are scarcely rivaled; because here is Terra Incognita: The Mind. ∎

TERRA INCOGNITA: THE MIND

by L. RON HUBBARD

P ROBABLY THE STRANGEST PLACE an explorer can go is inside. The earth's frontiers are being rapidly gobbled up by the fleet flight of planes. The stars are not yet reached. But there still exists a dark unknown which, if a strange horizon for an adventurer, is nevertheless capable of producing some adventures scarcely rivaled by Livingstone.

During the course of three minor expeditions before the war, the realization came about that one of the most dangerous risks in the field of exploration is not located in the vicinity of the geographical goal, but is hard by—from the first moment of planning until the last of disbanding—the unbalanced member of the party.

After some years of war it became even more of a conviction that there are some things more dangerous than the kamikaze, just as they had been more dangerous than malaria.

For a mathematician and navigator to become involved in the complexities of the mental frontiers is not particularly strange. To produce something like results from his explorations into the further realms of the unknown definitely is.

There is no reason here to become expansive on the subject of Dianetics. The backbone of the science can be found where it belongs, in the textbook and in professional publications on the mind and body.

But in that Dianetics was evolved because of observations in exploration for the purpose of bettering exploration results and safeguarding the success of expeditions, it would be strange, indeed, to make no mention of it in its proper generative field.

Based on heuristic principles and specifically on the postulate that the mission of life is survival and that the survival is in several lines rather than merely one, Dianetics contains several basic axioms which seem to approximate natural laws. But regardless of what it approximates, it works. Man surviving as himself, as his progeny, as his group or race, is still surviving equally well. The mechanisms of his body and his society are evidently intended to follow this axiom, since by following it in a scientific manner, several other discoveries came about. That Dianetics is of interest to medicine, in that it apparently conquers and cures all psychosomatic ills, and that it is of interest to institutions, where it has a salutary effect upon the insane, is beyond the province of its original intention.

What was wanted was a therapy which could be applied by expedition commanders or doctors which would work easily and in all cases to restore rationale to party members unduly affected by hardship and, more important, which would provide a yardstick in the selection of personnel which would obviate potential mental and physical failure. That goal was gained and, when gained, was found to be relatively simple.

"The earth's frontiers are being rapidly gobbled up by the fleet flight of planes. The stars are not yet reached. But there still exists a dark unknown..."

It was discovered that the human mind has not been too well credited for its actual ability. Rather than a weak and capricious organ, it was found to be inherently capable of amazing strength and stamina and that one of its primary purposes was to be right and always right. The normal mind can be restored to the optimum mind rather easily, but that is again beside the point.

The focus of infection of mental and psychosomatic ills was discovered in a hidden but relatively accessible place. During moments when the conscious mind (Dianetically, the "analytical mind") is suspended in operation (by injury, anesthesia, illness such as delirium), there is a more fundamental level still in operation, still recording. Anything said to a man when he is unconscious from pain or shock is registered in its entirety. It then operates, on the return of consciousness, as a posthypnotic suggestion, with the additional menace of holding in the body the pain of the incident. The content of the moment or period of unconsciousness is called, Dianetically, an "engram." The words contained in the engram are like commands, hidden but powerful when restimulated by an analogous situation in later life. The pain in the engram becomes the psychosomatic illness. Any perceptic in the engram is capable of reviving some of the strength of that engram when it is observed in the environment. The engram so planted in the mind has its content of perceptics—smell, sound, sight, tactile, organic sensations. It has them in a precise order. The engram can be played off like a drama when awake life perceptics restimulate it, which is to say that for every perceptic in the engram there are a variety of equivalents in awake environment. A man becomes weary, sees one or more of the perceptics in his surroundings and becomes subject to the engram within him.

For example, a man falls into a crevasse and is knocked out. His companions haul him forth. One is angry and comments over the unconscious man that he was always a clumsy fool and that the party would be better off without him. Another member defends the unconscious man, saying he is a good fellow. The unconscious man received a blow on the head in his fall, and his arm was slightly injured in the recovery.

After regaining consciousness the injured man has no "memory" of the incident, which is to say, he cannot recall it consciously. The incident may lie dormant and never become active. But for our example, the man who criticized him one day says, at the moment when the formerly injured man is weary, that somebody is a clumsy fool. Unreasonably, the formerly injured man will become intensely antagonistic. He will also feel an unreasonable friendship for the man who spoke up for him. Now the engram is *keyed-in* or has become a part of the subject's *behavior pattern*. The next time the injured man is on ice, the sight of it makes his head ache and his arm hurt in dwindling ratio to how tired he gets. Further, he may pick up a chronic headache or arthritis in his arm, the injuries being continually restimulated by such things as the smell of his parka, the presence of the other members, etc., etc.

That is an engram at work. How far it is capable of reducing a man's efficiency is a matter of many an explorer's log. A case of malaria can be restimulated. A man has malaria in a certain environment. Now having had it, he becomes far more susceptible to malaria *psychosomatically* in that same environment and with those people who tended him. He can become a serious drag on the party, for each new slight touch restimulates the old one, and what should have been a mild case is a highly painful one, being the first case of malaria plus all the subsequent cases. Malaria is a bug. As a bug it can be handled. As an engram it will defy cure, for there is no Atabrine for engrams, short of their removal.

> *"The focus of infection of mental and psychosomatic ills was discovered in a hidden but relatively accessible place."*

Almost all serious engrams occur early in life—amazingly early. The early ones form a basic structure to which it is very simple to append later engrams. Engrams can wait from childhood to be "keyed-in" and active at twenty-five, fifty, seventy years of age.

The engram, a period of unconsciousness which contained physical pain and apparent antagonism to the survival of the individual, has been isolated as the sole source of mental aberration. A certain part of the mind seems to be devoted to their reception and retention. In Dianetics, this part of the mind is called the "reactive mind." From this source, without otherwise disclosing themselves, the engrams act upon the body and cause the body to act in society in certain patterns. The reactive mind is alert during periods when the analytical mind (or conscious mind) is reduced in awareness.

It is a matter of clinical proof that the persistency, ambition, drive, willpower and personal force are in no degree dependent upon these engrams. The engram can only inhibit the natural drives. The value of this unconscious experience is valuable in an animal. It is a distinct liability to Man, who has outgrown his animal environment. The reactive mind, so long as it limits its activity to withdrawing, instinctively, a hand from a hot stove, is doing good service. With a vocabulary in it, it becomes deadly to the organism. Those familiar with general semantics will understand how the reactive mind computes when it is stated that it "computes" in identities. The word *horse* in the reactive mind may mean a headache, a broken leg and a scream. Such an engram, one containing these things, would be computed that a broken leg equals a scream, a scream a broken leg, a horse equals a scream, etc., etc. If the engram contained fright, then all these things are fright. The value of such a mental computation is entirely negative, inhibits the perfect calculations of which the analytical mind is capable and reduces the ability of the individual to be rational about, as noted, horses. Engrams also contain complimentary material which can bring about a manic state and which, again, is of slight use in computations.

The technique of Dianetics deletes from the reactive mind all engrams. They were hidden beneath layers of unconsciousness and unknown to the conscious mind before therapy. They were inhibitive to good impulses and productive of bad ones. After they are deleted by therapy, the conscious mind gains certain attributes it did not possess before, the individual is capable of greater efforts, his actual personality is greatly heightened and his ability to survive is enormously enhanced.

Engrams are contagious. A man has one he dramatizes as a rage pattern, and everyone has many. He dramatizes it while another individual is partly unconscious. The engram has now been implanted in the second individual.

Deletion of all engrams is practicable. The technique is relatively simple. There is little space here to give more than a most cursory glance at it, but an expedition commander can use it without any great knowledge of medicine and no other knowledge of psychiatry, which was the original goal at the beginning of research eleven years ago.

"...the individual is capable of greater efforts, his actual personality is greatly heightened and his ability to survive is enormously enhanced."

Therapy does not depend upon hypnosis. A state has been found which is much more desirable. Hypnosis is amnesia trance for the purpose of planting suggestions. The problem of hypnosis is to put the patient to sleep. The purpose of the Dianetic reverie is to wake the patient up. Narcosynthesis and other drug therapies have some slight use in Dianetics. But the primary technique consists of stimulants. The best stimulant is Benzedrine. In its absence an overdose of coffee will do.

The patient is made to lie down and shut his eyes. The operator begins to count. He suggests the patient relax. At length the patient's eyelids will flutter. (Medicine drumming will also accomplish this without producing a harmful amnesia hypnotic state.) He is permitted to relax further. Then the operator tells him that his *motor strip* (his sensory perceptions) is returning to a time of unconsciousness, the time being specifically named. With coaxing, the patient will begin to feel the injury and sense himself in the location and time of the accident. He is then asked to recount all that happened, word for word, feeling by feeling. He is asked to do this several times, each time being "placed back" at the beginning of the incident. The period of unconsciousness he experienced then should begin to lighten and he can at length recount everything which went on when he was unconscious. It is necessary that he feel and see everything in the period of unconsciousness each time he recounts the incident. Nothing is said about his being able to remember and no hypnoanalysis technique is used. He merely recounts it until he cannot longer feel any pain in it, until he is entirely cheerful about it. Then he is brought to present time by just that command and told to again recount the incident. He may have to do this twice or three times in present time, for the somatic pains will again have returned. The treatment is repeated two days later. All feeling of injury from it and all aberrative factors in the incident will vanish.

This technique is outlined here for use on a patient who is not *cleared* of engrams prior to this new accident. A Dianetic Clearing from the first unconsciousness of a lifetime to the present time places a man in a situation which is almost injury- and aberration-proof.

The emergency aspect of this technique is valuable. Clinical tests have shown that when shock is Dianetically removed immediately after an injury, the rate of healing is enormously accelerated, so much so that burns have healed in a few hours. Malaria and various fevers, when their peak effects are Dianetically removed, improve with great speed.

Incidents of hardship and deprivation can be markedly lightened in the recovery period by removing their psychic shock.

It is quite remarkable that the various manifestations and "cures" of native witchcraft and shamanism can be uniformly duplicated and bettered by a modern science like Dianetics. An engram can bring about a mental hallucination (with a simple command like "You can only listen to me!") which gives a "demon" aspect. The individual containing such an engram would be considered by a shaman to have within him a demon, for the demon is the only sonic memory the individual would have.

While Dianetics does not consider the brain as an electronic computing machine except for purposes of analogy, it is nevertheless a member of that class of sciences to which belong general semantics and cybernetics and, as a matter of fact, forms a bridge between the two. There can be as many engramic commands as there can be words in a language and as many engramic injuries as there can be illnesses and accidents. Therefore it is no surprise that circuits can be set up in the brain which approximate any school of witchcraft, shamanism and religion known to Man. The Banks Islander sitting around talking to his deceased relatives and getting answers would be found, on examination, to have a fine array of engrams and a very active reactive mind.

"...when shock is Dianetically removed immediately after an injury, the rate of healing is enormously accelerated, so much so that burns have healed in a few hours."

The selection of personnel who will not be subject to sullen or hostile behavior and who will not become ill under various climatic conditions depends in a large measure on the perceptions of the individual. If an individual can recall things he has heard by simply hearing them again (audio imagery), if he can recall things he has seen simply by seeing them again, in color, in his mind (visio imagery), if he can imagine in terms of color-visio and tone-audio (imagine in terms of color motion pictures with sound) and if he can recall his father and mother as of early childhood, the chances are very good that he will prove to be a very stable man. Additionally, he should prove to be, within the limits of his intelligence and physical being, an able man. Unfortunately, such persons are quite rare.

If a man has definite anger patterns, worries about things and has unthinking prejudices, he may prove difficult, for these are the outward manifestations of a large reactive mind.

Taking a man back into a geographical area where he has many times been may be profitable from an experience standpoint, but a record of accidents and misadventures in that area would be a definite point of consideration. While it would not mean entirely that a man was a bad risk, there is a double factor involved. He might have had his accidents because he contained a variety of engrams which commanded that he have accidents (the accident-prone is the extreme case). And having had accidents in the area, he probably gained several engrams there which would reduce his efficiency in that area.

A man whose service, in point of experience, would be invaluable to an expedition might be, in point of potential aberration, a risk to that expedition. There is a remedy for such a valuable man: he can be cleared of his engrams, in which case his past record of accidents and failures becomes entirely invalid as a criteria for future conduct.

Dianetics has been variously tested and has been found to work uniformly and predictably in all cases. There are many more aspects to it than have been elucidated here, but it is possible to use just these facts to obtain excellent results. In a true, complete erasure of past moments of unconsciousness, the engram disappears utterly. In the above case it will probably only alleviate, return slightly in three days and then reduce to a null level of reaction and stay that way, no longer affecting the patient.

The science has the virtue that it can be worked by any intelligent man after only a few weeks of study. That is, for the entire art of *Clearing* a case. An intelligent man could learn all he needed to know about alleviation of a case in a few hours of reading.

> *"The science has the virtue that it can be worked by any intelligent man after only a few weeks of study."*

The original goal was to provide expedition commanders and doctors with a therapy tool which would increase the efficiency of personnel and reduce incidence of personnel failure. Dianetics, after eleven years of research and testing, bit off a trifle more than it had bargained for. There had been no intention to go holistic and solve the ills of Mankind. That it began to cure psychosomatic illnesses such as arthritis, migraine, ulcers, coronary, asthma, frostbite, bursitis, allergies, etc., etc., that it did quick things about mental derangement on the institutional level and began to replace that strange barbarism, the prefrontal lobotomy, was entirely outside the initial scheme of research. That it would now sail off on a new course to chase down the cause of cancer and cure it was not on the chart.

If it does these things, as it appears to be doing, it is in the medical and psychiatric province. No such intentions existed when the terra incognita of the mind was explored for its answers. It was intended as a tool for the expedition commander and doctor who are faced with choosing personnel and maintaining that personnel in good health. It is hoped that to these it will be of good value. If it is not, then despite acclaim, it will in some measure have failed. *Ron*

The eminent author of *Dianetics,* as he appeared to readers in the spring of 1950

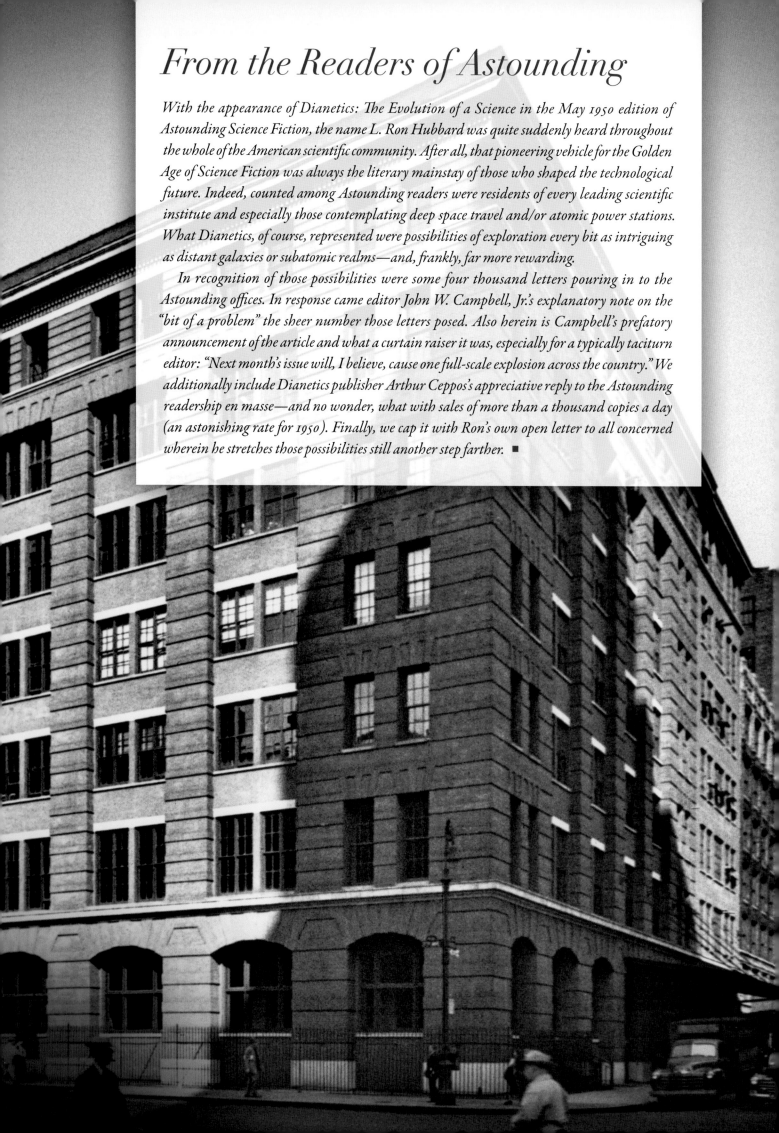

From the Readers of Astounding

With the appearance of Dianetics: The Evolution of a Science in the May 1950 edition of Astounding Science Fiction, the name L. Ron Hubbard was quite suddenly heard throughout the whole of the American scientific community. After all, that pioneering vehicle for the Golden Age of Science Fiction was always the literary mainstay of those who shaped the technological future. Indeed, counted among Astounding readers were residents of every leading scientific institute and especially those contemplating deep space travel and/or atomic power stations. What Dianetics, of course, represented were possibilities of exploration every bit as intriguing as distant galaxies or subatomic realms—and, frankly, far more rewarding.

In recognition of those possibilities were some four thousand letters pouring in to the Astounding offices. In response came editor John W. Campbell, Jr.'s explanatory note on the "bit of a problem" the sheer number those letters posed. Also herein is Campbell's prefatory announcement of the article and what a curtain raiser it was, especially for a typically taciturn editor: "Next month's issue will, I believe, cause one full-scale explosion across the country." We additionally include Dianetics publisher Arthur Ceppos's appreciative reply to the Astounding readership en masse—and no wonder, what with sales of more than a thousand copies a day (an astonishing rate for 1950). Finally, we cap it with Ron's own open letter to all concerned wherein he stretches those possibilities still another step farther. ∎

SCIENCE FICTION

IN TIMES TO COME

Next month's issue will, I believe, cause one full-scale explosion across the country. We are carrying a sixteen thousand word article entitled "Dianetics...An Introduction to a New Science," by L. Ron Hubbard. It will, I believe, be the first publication of the material. It is, I assure you in full and absolute sincerity, one of the most important articles ever published. In this article, reporting on Hubbard's own research into the engineering question of how the human mind operates, immensely important basic discoveries are related. Among them:

A technique of psychotherapy has been developed which will cure *any* insanity not due to organic destruction of the brain.

A technique that gives any man a perfect, indelible, total memory, and perfect, errorless ability to compute his problems.

A basic answer, and a technique for curing—not alleviating—ulcers, arthritis, asthma, and many other nongerm diseases.

A totally new conception of the truly incredible ability and power of the human mind.

Evidence that insanity is contagious, and *is not hereditary*.

This is no wild theory. It is not mysticism. It is a coldly precise engineering description of how the human mind operates, and how to go about restoring correct operation tested and used on some two hundred fifty cases. And it makes only one overall claim: the methods logically developed from that description *work*. The memory stimulation technique is so powerful that, within thirty minutes of entering therapy, most people will recall in full detail their own birth. I have observed it in action, and used the techniques myself.

I leave it to your judgment: Will such an article be of interest to you? It is not only a fact article of the highest importance; it is the story of the ultimate adventure—an exploration in the strangest of all *terra incognita;* the human mind. No stranger adventure appeared in the Arabian Nights than Hubbard's experience, using his new techniques, in plowing through the strange jungle of distorted thoughts within a human mind. To find, beyond that zone of madness, a computing mechanism of ultimate and incredible efficiency and perfection! To find that a fully sane, enormously able and altruistic personality is trapped deep in every human mind—however insane or criminal it may appear on the outside!

The Editor
ASTOUNDING SCIENCE FICTION

Left Street & Smith, publishers, New York City; home of *Astounding Science Fiction*

"One's necessary before you can join the Service. I'll fly the machine."

The gale lifted them high and the wire thrummed with the force of the wind. There was a moment of awful movement as Ted released the tow ring and then they were riding the storm.

"Now to land her without crashing," said Mary.

"I shall do that safely on Headquarters landing field," said Ted grinning, "but it will be a most almighty thump!"

It was.

THE END.

IMES TO COME

...r by Brush, familiar heretofore on the inside art work; ...ver by Miller, who illustrates—or perhaps it would be ...bbard's dianetics article in this issue. Each is new on the ...f interest and help. I think you'll like Miller's cover next ...u'll like the story it illustrates—Katherine MacLean's

...se, be Part III of "Wizard of Linn"; van Vogt, as usual, ...that section. It's a rather important point he makes—one ...d has been overloooked in many science-fiction stories. ...to ruin, the ruins don't settle uniformly, forming a regu- ...ound. When a great culture collapses—would every piece ...ree, in the same way, at the same rate? That can make ...ial results!

...ing up by J. J. Coupling, called "How To Build a Think- ...it-diagrams, and exact descriptions of a relatively sim- ...think. It will learn, remember, and forget. But the most ...upling's extremely strong argument that the ideal think- ...following characteristics.

...y the first time it experiences something.

...rderly fashion!

...aining patterns indelibly—it must be able to "forget" to

...points sound entirely the reverse of an ideal thinking ...g argument Coupling presents is intriguing indeed. ...June issue, incidentally, but follows soon.

THE EDITOR.

DIANETICS | THE EVOLUTION OF A SCIENCE

BY L. RON HUBBARD

A fact article of genuine importance. See the Editor's Page.

Illustrated by Miller

INTRODUCTION

The editor asked me to write this introduction to one of the most important articles ever to be published in Astounding SCIENCE FICTION, for some very good reasons. First, he wanted to make certain that you readers would *not* confuse Dianetics with thiotimoline or with any other bit of scientific spoofing. This is too important to be misinterpreted. Second, he wanted to demonstrate that the medical profession—or at least part of it—was not only aware of the science of Dianetics, but had tested its tenets and techniques, and was willing to admit that there was something to it.

There *is* something to it; there is so much to it, in fact, that its potentialities cannot yet be fully comprehended. Those of us who have worked with Dianetics—and that includes the Editor—have seen what it can do, and are convinced of its tremendous importance. I am not going to try to persuade you of its importance to you personally and to the human race; you must determine that for yourself. But while you are exercising your judicious, scientific skepticism, let me give you another point to consider in the meantime.

Dianetics is, in addition to all its other attributes, a thrilling adventure. Ron Hubbard, long a member of the Explorers Club, has gone exploring in the most obscure *terra incognita* of all—the human mind. He has explored a region wherein lies the mightiest power in the known Universe.

The mightiest power known in the Universe today is not the atomic bomb; that power was discovered, developed and controlled by the greater power of human thought. And human thought—our most intimate possession—has been the least known of all powers. Hubbard, in undertaking this research, undertook the greatest adventure any man can imagine—a stranger and more fantastic experience than any visit to the cities of the Arabian Nights. To understand the human mind, he had to find a path into the seat of madness, find a way through that zone of distortion of thought—and on the other side he found the most marvelous mechanism imaginable. He found a computing machine, whose functional capacities tran-

43

Dianetics: The Evolution of a Science as originally published in the May 1950 edition of *Astounding Science Fiction* and inspiring some two thousand inquiring letters in the space of two weeks

ASTOUNDING
SCIENCE FICTION

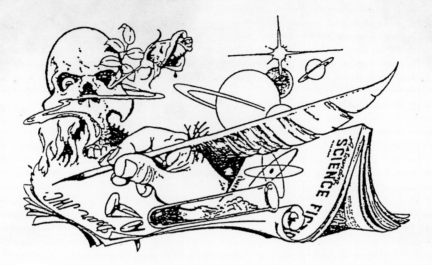

BRASS TACKS

From the Editor:

We encounter a bit of a problem. Most of the letters this month were, of course, concerned with Dianetics. Since some two thousand of them arrived during the first two weeks, nearly all going to Hermitage House ordering the book, it is a little difficult to present a sampling. Some 0.2 percent were unfavorable; to be a true sampling, I would have to run one of those and some five hundred of the others—which is slightly impractical. And it is impossible for us to answer many of the questioning letters, because of sheer volume. Therefore Hubbard, and Arthur Ceppos of Hermitage House, are answering in the only possible way—herewith. And I regret, but with a two thousand letter Brass Tacks, the problem becomes impossible!

Dear Mr. Campbell:

This is, truly astounding, Dianetics!

One sunny afternoon at seven thousand feet in the flak-shredded air over Dieppe, I looked over my left shoulder across two hundred yards of open space and watched the dancing devils of flame spurt from the leading edge of the wings of an FW-190, knowing that each flash might well be my last impression in this life as I busied myself with the mechanics of getting out of the line of fire in my little Spitfire.

And on another sunny morning in French Morocco, I "drove" my P-39 over the brow of a low hill at roughly three hundred miles per hour and dipped its nose to find an unmapped hi-tension line directly in my path, to feel the hot breath of Hell in the shock and flash that followed, and to wonder—seriously—if I had lived through the experience, even as I did so.

I've weaved and dodged the vicious, impersonal black bursts of antiaircraft fire over France and the Channel, trying not to guess when or whether the lads on the earth below would load the shell with "my number" on it.

I've flown my P-400 over thirteen hundred miles of open ocean from England to Africa—seven hours and a quarter strapped in a seat midway between heaven and a cold and watery interment, knowing that the odds on my reaching Port Lyautey were considerably less than even.

I have explored the middle and upper reaches of the notorious Casbah of Algiers in the hours between midnight and four A.M., armed, of course, but accompanied by two men in allied uniforms and a "French" civilian all of whom were unknown to me as late as eleven-thirty that same evening.

I watched the dust and debris rise to fifteen thousand feet or more over the little island of Pantelleria under the terrible power of salvoed bombs from massed B-17s.

I've made at least five hundred landings in fighter aircraft of one kind or another, each one a separate little problem in survival.

And I could go on and on and on, but shall belabor you no further. My point is that I have some reason to believe that I have had at least my share of experience of and of opportunity to plumb the depths and explore the heights of feeling attainable by earthlings.

But nothing I have ever done, read, heard, seen, felt or sensed in any way has affected me as profoundly as this material on Dianetics. For the very first time, I find myself justified in the use of words like awesome, electrifying, earth-shaking, etc.

If this new word does indeed represent a new Science—as you and your writers have described it—then your name along with Hubbard's belongs to History.

Harry J. Robb,
625 Ray Avenue, N. W.,
New Philadelphia, Ohio.

Dear Mr. Campbell:

I read L. Ron Hubbard's article "Dianetics" with great interest, and have placed an order for his book.

Hubbard briefly mentioned Political Dianetics, Industrial Dianetics and other potential divisions of this new mental science. As a student teacher of United States History I am interested in the ramifications of Educational Dianetics.

For a time I majored in psychology and soon came to regard its present state as very provisional and incomplete: something like that of medicine during the Middle Ages. (The professionalization in this field—Ph. D. requirements for clinical psychologists, and the like—is no proof of its scientific nature. Medieval students had to carefully study the Four Humors and other erroneous doctrines before receiving their degrees.) Hence this new approach in psychology has stirred my interest and hopes.

For the last two years, while taking my required teacher-training courses, I have come to believe that the present methods of education are inefficient even when fortified with stiff doses of audio-visual technique. We—generally speaking—are crammed with all sorts of technical knowledge and psychological principles and practices. But our mental capacities remain essentially unchanged. We can't remember all the data pumped into us or convert our psychological lore into brilliant practice. In short, our mental level remains at about ten to twenty percent of total capacity. Library reference skills, refresher courses, private libraries of texts and audio-visual aids are indifferent substitutes for full mental utilization. If Dianetics can increase utilization of our mental capacities, it will do more for education than all the other techniques before mentioned.

Wallace Liggett,
1865 Euclid Avenue,
Berkeley 9, California.

Dear Mr. Campbell:

We would like to express through your columns our appreciation of your readers' response to Dianetics.

Although no major advertising or publicity campaign has been entered upon by our firm at this date, "Dianetics: The Modern Science of Mental Health: Handbook of Therapy" is selling at the rate of about one thousand copies per day. We have been receiving from one hundred and fifty to three hundred and fifty orders a day, cash in advance, from the readers of Astounding SCIENCE FICTION alone.

We have been pleasantly amazed at the quality of the letters received by us from your readers. There is a preponderance of professional men within your readership obviously. About five percent of the orders we have received because of your magazine have been from medical doctors. A much higher percentage has been from engineers and college professors.

It is hoped that your readers will excuse us the delay in forwarding copies in response to orders. The author is partially responsible for this delay for he worked until the very last moment to make certain that every scrap of information about Dianetics which would be of use was included in the handbook and that no major problem of therapy was left uncovered. Even so, this has been a record time of publication from the moment of receipt of the manuscript to the finished product.

Our general and national publicity on Dianetics will begin shortly. In the interim, your reader response has been magnificent. We have been considerably impressed by the intelligence of the letters we have received and by the persons of those readers who called personally at our offices to reserve a book.

Arthur Ceppos,
President, Hermitage House,
One Madison Avenue,
New York City.

That delay was caused by the addition of nearly fifty thousand additional words of material.

Dear Readers:

I would like to express my deep appreciation for the magnificent response given to the article *Dianetics: The Evolution of a Science*.

Over two thousand letters arrived in the offices of this magazine and Hermitage House in New York, the publishers of the *Handbook*. As the letters are still arriving as this is written, at the rate of more than two hundred per day, I cannot say with accuracy what the total response will be. Less than fifteen of these letters were adversely critical and only three were thoroughly agin Dianetics. In that one of the three was from a young gentleman who was on the verge of receiving his master's degree in psychology, the bitterness of the letter is easy to understand and one is rather moved to feel sympathy with the writer. A score of two thousand in favor to three against rather tends to swallow up the opposition and to carry out a principle I have often noted, that the wild protests against Dianetics forecast by some of its supporters fail to materialize as soon as an accurate knowledge of it is communicated.

The publication of the article seems to have saved several lives. And it has gained very considerable report for the new science. Over fifty medical doctors and psychiatrists wrote letters couched in terms of high approval. Not one single individual whose profession was intimately connected with mental work and who was experienced with it found fault with Dianetics. Indeed, it seems that those who best understand, through professional work, the problems of the mind are those who most readily grasp and accept Dianetics. The roll call of professionals intensely interested in Dianetics now contains some of the most prominent authorities on the mind in the United States.

The enthusiasm of response has been most gratifying. Dianetics seems to have taken off like several V-2 rockets in a bundle but, we hope, with a more constructive purpose.

It would be quite beyond me as a matter of sheer labor to answer the many queries on specific points which were contained in some of the letters. No point advanced in any of these letters is not covered in the Handbook. The article was, of necessity, brief and sketchy in spots. In the 180,000 words of the Handbook, adequate coverage is given to all points. Of course some of the letters were answered because they had an emergency status. Example: "I am contemplating suicide. Can Dianetics help me?" Example: "I have for some time considered the commission of a murder. What can Dianetics do for me that will make it unnecessary?" Example: "My baby is about to be born. What can I do to make the birth easier?" Dianetics can help in each case, certainly.

One reader commented that while the article changed things for him radically, buses still ran and *Time* had not mentioned it. Actually *Time* will shortly devote space to Dianetics, as has *Pathfinder*. This magazine, *Astounding Science Fiction,* got what the newspapermen call a *beat*. Few national publications, in the next few months, will not carry stories on Dianetics, space having been arranged for by them in the past two months. No national publicity beyond a science item in *Pathfinder* and the article in *Astounding* has been released as of this writing.

Several readers seemed to be interested in how Dianetics stood in relationship to God and the Infinite Mind. Some assumed that it proved Man's spirituality, some assumed that it disproved it. Dianetics is in the same position as physics in relation to God and the Infinite Mind. While it may make a clear view of this problem possible, it does not in any way pretend to either deny a man a soul or to endow him with one. Whatever my personal opinions are on this matter have no place in Dianetics, for Dianetics does not depend upon opinion, neither mine nor the opinion of some authority on religion or mysticism. Dianetics is constructed to be used and to be used by anyone in any frame of reference. It should not become a bone of contention as to what it proves or disproves in fields which it is not trying to enter.

A general query, contained both in the letters and conversations I have had lately with various readers of this magazine, has to do with how one overcomes opposition to Dianetics on the part of one's friends. Evidently many individuals have attempted to communicate Dianetics to others who, knowing nothing about it, have simply refused to receive any knowledge of it, primarily on the grounds that the problem of the human mind is terribly complicated and cannot be solved and that therefore it is of no use to listen to any possible solution.

Apropos of this matter, let us take the case of a writer for this magazine who, ten months ago, elected himself a violent opponent of Dianetics. No release of its tenets had been made and he knew nothing whatever about  it. But he was opposed to it. Four months later he engaged in violent argument with a medical doctor who was supporting Dianetics. Four months after that he was savage in his denouncement of Dianetics. But in midflight the isolated datum came home to him that a ringing in the ears was a psychosomatic condition. Immediately he stopped resistance long enough to ask what would cause the three-thousand-cycle note. He was told that it was possibly a quinine abortion attempt, with his mother saying, "It just won't stop. My ears go on ringing and ringing and ringing until I'm almost crazy." A few hours after that he was on the phone begging for some data about Dianetic therapy. In short, opposition generally comes from a complete ignorance of the subject and an unwillingness to inspect it. Further, opposition to Dianetics breaks down instantly when the opposer realizes that he, himself, personally has a stake in it. After that the opposition vanishes.

Some of the auditors here have developed a method of "selling Dianetics" which they term "showing yard goods." They do not try to sell it at all, but if a person is interested, they will answer his questions. Dianetics actually doesn't have to be sold. The psychology professor who was reported by one reader to have used his entire hour in scathing denunciation of that "trash" knew nothing about Dianetics, had made no tests, had read no data or Axioms and was generally uninformed about the subject. If that professor were to qualify as a scientist, he would have to lay aside such extreme emotionalism, for science is a  matter of facts, not of opinions. The reader reporting it, evidently one of the students, was rendered extremely curious as to just what direction that professor's aberrations were taking him. Nevertheless, if the man were to be given data on Dianetics and persuaded into a cool survey of them, it is certain that his attitude would alter, for Dianetics shapes up in the form of laboratory tests as prettily as you please and is, indeed, the experimental system the psychologist needed in order to qualify himself as an exact scientist and to render him immune from the brickbats which are continually being pitched at him by the physical scientist. Dianetics places the psychologist in a very firm position, for he can prove that what he is working upon has great value and has, additionally, precision in its results. Using Dianetics, the psychologist is safe from such a bombast as he was given in the recent book, *Science Is a Sacred Cow*. Dianetics is on his side. If he or anyone else wants to attack it, that's a God-given right. If anyone wants to use it or needs it, he will see it.

Almost all opposition to Dianetics comes from ignorance of it and folds up (except when one is dealing with a truly moronic mind or a psychotic) the moment the details and evidences of the science are surveyed.

It is to be remembered too that many individuals have a stake in past methods and theories relating to the mind and that such individuals see in Dianetics an economic threat or a threat to personal prestige. One must be able to appreciate and understand this. Usually the size of the stake and the damage Dianetics will do to somebody's paycheck are both fantasies. Personally I have met very few such people. But when I have, in a few days or a few months they have responded favorably. Remember that some minds are not as swift in grasping things as others and that some minds are so engrossed in personal prestige and economics that they do not see benefit in anything which will not serve these fixations.

The very best method of convincing anyone about Dianetics is to let him ease down his own time track and discover a few things. In other words, give him what we call a *short run* in therapy. It can't hurt him. It usually predisposes him to a pleased wonder about this new horizon and even enthusiastic participation in Dianetics.

Above all, don't worry about whether people accept Dianetics or not. A majority opinion does not necessarily establish the truth of anything. For instance, the fact that the enlightened of Shakespeare's time may have believed in ghosts did not prove that ghosts existed. Individual opinion is valid only after observation of something. If a man won't observe, forget him.

A strange thing is happening and will continue to happen. There is a direct ratio between the brilliance of a mind and its ability to understand and work Dianetics. We have proven that continually. A person highly successful, for instance, in the field of psychoanalysis can be counted upon to grasp Dianetics quickly. The second-rater,

whose practice is unsuccessful, whose security is already small, may have difficulty in understanding Dianetics and even be savage about it. Out of this comes, whatever we do or might wish to do to prevent it, an aristocracy of the mind. People who are bright and have a high dynamic, understanding and undergoing Clearing, will become brighter and will have a higher dynamic. There will be many of these. But they will have to carry on their own energy, so to speak, those that they wish to benefit. Below this will be the persons whose insanity or criminality has made them a menace to society (and who will be given a *Release* in Dianetics at state cost) and those persons who have money enough to buy a Release or a Clear—expensive when not done in teams, as no good professional practitioner would work for less than $15 an hour and usually charge more. On a lower strata there will be those who for various reasons do not undertake Clearing and for whom no Clearing is done. A wide gulf is thereby established. On the adage that "them as has, *gits*," one sees with some sadness that more than three-quarters of the world's population will become subject to the remaining quarter as a natural consequence and about which we can do exactly nothing. The saving part of this is that the good will of the upper quarter will inhibit their exploitation of the less fortunate.

So if your friend or relative turns his back on Dianetics and refuses to inspect it even after you have done your best to explain it, don't be disheartened. That you see it and can use it has not injured him in any way. The loss is definitely his, not yours.

A further word. Many of you will have the book at the time you read this. I call your attention to the fact that so long as you use standard technique without diluting it with hypnosis or drugs or some preconception, you are utterly and entirely safe, your patient is safe and nothing whatever can happen that will injure anyone. A long, long series of experiments has demonstrated this. Any case is better opened than left closed, even when the auditor is entirely unskilled. So feel no apprehensions about what you might do or what is being done to you, just keep following the rules as closely as you can.

We are opening an institute for training professional auditors because so many psychiatrists and psychoanalysts and medical doctors have expressed a desire for special training. Probably institutes will be opened in various parts of the country as soon as we get around to it. A Foundation has been formed for the control of such institutes—and the proceeds of the Handbook, by the way, have been given in their entirety to the Foundation—and it is only a question of time before one will be in your neighborhood if all goes well. However, this should not inhibit your practicing as per the Handbook in any way, nor even practicing professionally if you will.

Please accept my thanks, again, for your blazing reception of Dianetics, for your compliments and congratulations. They amply reward a score of years of hard labor.

L. Ron Hubbard

DIANETICS

THE MODERN SCIENCE OF MENTAL HEALTH

A HANDBOOK OF DIANETIC THERAPY

L. RON HUBBARD

DIANETICS

THE MODERN SCIENCE OF MENTAL HEALTH

L. RON HUBBARD

ERMITAGE

CHAPTER THREE

Letters from the
EYE OF THE STORM

Letters from the
Eye of the Storm

"I had that book on Dianetics to get out and it went about 180,000 words," remarked LRH to Russell Hays in the wonderfully offhand and slow-drawl style punctuating all Hubbard-Hays correspondence. Also appearing in a cameo role through letters from these days is the legendary Robert Heinlein. He was likewise expecting to receive a copy of said book on Dianetics. "Or do I expect too much?" Not at all, Ron replies, but admittedly demands on his time were unrelenting. To wit: these were additionally days when a first Dianetic Research Foundation came to fruition, inspiring visions of desks stretching out interminably and paper storms of wafting memoranda. Meanwhile, both *Time* and the *New York Times* had slotted features on the subject. Then there were the "skillion other magazines" requesting coverage, while national columnist Walter Winchell had just declared: "There is something new coming up in April called Dianetics. A new science which works with the invariability of physical science in the field of the human mind. From all indications it will prove to be as revolutionary for humanity as the first caveman's discovery and utilization of fire."

The point, as newspaper headlines would soon proclaim: "Dianetics—Taking U.S. by Storm."

Still, it is probably difficult to appreciate just how intense was that storm (particularly in an age when Dianetics has become so utterly

Below
"There is something new coming up in April called Dianetics"
—American newspaper columnist and radio personality Walter Winchell

Left With students of a first Hubbard Dianetic Research Foundation, 1950

pervasive, one imagines it was always so). But the fact is, when journalists pronounced it America's "fastest growing movement" and cited associations that "blossomed like wild flowers in the spring," the statements were not exaggerated in the least. Nor was Ron exaggerating when referencing a storm of letters from readers, an equally demanding flurry of requests for instruction and lectures and—once more jocularly to Hays—the "wild-eyed enthusiasts keep comin' round and makin' my weekends miserable." Nonetheless, he attended to all: lecturing and instructing five days a week, graciously receiving those who banged at his New Jersey door on Saturdays and Sundays and—as evidenced here—dutifully responding to a veritable avalanche of inquiries from interested parties all over hither and yon.

Obviously, only a fraction of those letters have been reprinted here. Included in the sampling is an impassioned note from a Vivian Shirley, among the first of those "wild-eyed enthusiasts." Also included is an equally poignant appeal from one Frank Dessler who begs for a chance to experience Dianetics (and would, in fact, latterly serve as a top executive in the Hubbard Dianetic Research Foundation of Los Angeles). Finally, we offer a succinct but telling LRH reply to one Otto Gabler of R. E. Scott Company charged with leasing Ron's temporary quarters on Aberdeen Road. It seems objections were lodged to the volume of traffic illegally blocking access to neighboring driveways. But, of course, when one is about to meet the author of *Dianetics,* who the hell cares about a parking ticket? ■

Bay Head NJ 2 Apr. 50

Dear Russkell;

I been meaning to indict you an eepistle here for some time but I had that book on Dianetics to get out and it went about 180,000 words and then I just got rid of a 50,000 word novel and between times these wild-eyed enthusiasts keep comin' round and makin' my weekends miserable and I'd give one heell of a lot, my good friend, even for a snoose of snuff and some vile Kansas beer. Lately they had a book called No Place To Hide. Well, that's me, brother, and it's gettin' worse quick. Pathfinder carries the first release on Apr. 6. AP releasing their story shortly. TIME and the NY TIMES both carrying a long story on Dianetics. Then Ast. Science Fiction. Ads in Publishers Weekly, been in Winchell, requests from Satevepost, Scientific American for review copies and about a skillion other magazines.

Things been happening. For instance a guy called up and said his wife was dying in a NY hospital. A doctor went up in a hurry, found out they'd given her up in both psychiatry and medicine and the priests were spreading their palms for the last rites. He brought her out of a chronic colitis, which was what was killing her, in exactly four hours of therapy. She had left the hospital and a week after treatment has gained twelve pounds, keeps gaining at ½ lb. per day, is walking and talking and working and feeling wonderful. This impressed hell out of the press. Couple other random cases, just as spectacular. About thirty regular therapies going on at present, none of them I've met, all of whom are advancing swiftly. Washington School of Psychiatry will probably adopt it as a standard therapy, etc.

Hoping this will apprise you of developments and hoping you are the same—

best regards,
Ron

Bay Head NJ 28 Mar 50

Dear Bob, dearest Ginny;

Thank you for the congrats. My heartiest hopes for your own publishing efforts.

It's about 2:00 AM—0200 to you! 4 bells as my clock just rang. Cat just came over to see who I was writing and to steal my eraser.

Going to have to send you one of my first batch of books. Galleys being poured back at the printer in a stream. No extras. 180,000 word ms begun Jan. 12, '50, finished Feb. 10, off the press by April 25. Some going by all hands. Would have been a disservice to you to send anything but a fully comprehensive work. The present work was written, on the advice of Spinoza, in the language of the people. It was not tailored for professional psychiatry since it has nothing in common with it save that it applies to the mind. Only criticism from PSYCHIATRY and psychiatrists is that it may be a method only the originator can work. There are thirty patients currently being treated in this area whom I have never seen and who are showing excellent progress. Anybody getting cleared by this very limited group of auditors does so in the understanding that he or she will clear somebody else. We believe the book will give enough data to permit the normally intelligent to start right in without help. Sharpies like you shouldn't have any trouble.

Things are humming along. Eleven years of quiet research are exploding into something which seems to be well accepted. But carrying this load, financing it personally, working hard on it and doing my own work besides makes me long for the long sea rolling and the lift of a heeling deck. The Isles of Greece, the Isles of Greece. Joisey, frankly, bores me.

Love,
Ron

1825 Cheyenne Blvd.,
Colorado Springs, Colo.

17 April 1950

Dear Ron,

Your letter of 28 March indicates that your book on Dianetics will be off the press on 25 April. Therefore I shall get up a bit early on 26 April, expecting to receive it by air mail special delivery. Or do I expect too much?

Honestly, I can hardly wait to read the thing. I have had just enough in the way of tastes of the matter from the proofs of the article for Astounding, from your letters and from John's letters, to make me extremely anxious to sit down and read a long organized continuous account of the matter. So please do not delay unnecessarily in sending me a copy.

No real news here. We are both well and happy and very busy with our house building plans. When we get the house finished, I still hope to make that trip East. I hope that you will not have departed somewhere beyond the horizon before we get there, or if you do start to travel, you should include Colorado in your wanderings.

Our best to you,
Bob and Ginny

Dear Irrepressible Combination;

We had a press conference in Dianetics Wednesday. Didn't realize until I got there that when a major publisher throws a conference he means it. Drinks and luncheon for thirty major publications and news services some of which had more than one representing. TIMES, LIFE, TIME, FORTUNE, SCI AM, TOMORROW, AP, etc. etc. I still feel on Friday like I've been riding a PC bridge in the Bering, flank speed. Two psychiatrists there, both beginning very skeptical and ending with a couple hurrahs and quite embarrassing me. Everybody called it the best conference they'd been at for years.

I am having a first copy sent at you by the publisher. And I enclose the release that was handed out at the conference. The superlatives are the publisher's.

The publisher and Campbell and a few more have whipped up the HUBBARD DIANETIC RESEARCH FOUNDATION which is complete except for capital and a bunch of ivy-covered walls and I can just see those desks stretching out and the organizational memoranda and Mrs. Swilch who has five thousand diamonds and a cough sitting there telling me about the ailments of her Pekingese.

The standard therapy technique has been proven adequate in the hands of people who have not been treated by me, the book tells all, the publisher and the boys in the foundation are all on the job, the press releases are about to break in earnest. And my god it looks dull around here! I haven't touched a patient for weeks except for a couple casual check-ups. The trouble with doing anything for society is that society thinks you do it for plaudits and expect to strut around and wear laurel on the brow or something equally idiotic. Dianetic therapy leads straight to Homo Novis, and the world gets to look so bright it's like dawn when you were a kid. I'm as restless as a sailor on the edge of ten quart creek ten thousand miles inland.

All my love,
Ron

Right Hermitage House, original publisher of *Dianetics* and then situated in New York's Metropolitan Life Tower

April 20, 1950

Mr. L. Ron Hubbard
c/o Astounding Science Fiction
New York, N.Y.

Dear Mr. Hubbard,

I have waited twenty-four hours to write you so that there would be an interval for my enthusiasm after reading your article on "Dianetics" to cool. It hasn't. And I'm still in a state of blissful contemplation of an unfolding universe. Today I will buy the book and begin the study but:

If Dianetics is the kind of technique you describe, one would need a special kind of technical training to meet the demands of the service it can render. I would like to be trained to be such a technician. How can I do it?

I have an excellent background for special training, teaching in high school, newspaper woman with a signed column (seven years), syndication, marriage, two children, freelancing, then public relations; I was director of Public Relations for the New York State Commission against Discrimination for two and a half years. Last year I did research in modern psychology and ghosted some mss for a psychological consultant.

Right now I am at a fork in the road. I have been considering the possibility of trying for a doctorate in psychology with the intention of becoming a psychological consultant but my experience last year did not convince me of the efficacy of the methods now in use; they seemed palliative rather than conducive to a complete cure.

Now Dianetics appears; it sounds like the answer for me in regard to the four drives you outlined in the astounding article: (please note: no quotes on astounding.)

Sincerely
Vivian Shirley

May 10, 1950

Dear Mr. Hubbard;

Please do not treat this letter lightly. To you it may sound a bit juvenile and you will probably receive many letters pro and con. But to me your article in Astounding was the most important thing I have ever read. "Dianetics" is so new and startling that the mind has difficulty digesting all of it.

Although I am far from being young, having reached the age of forty, I am and have been pondering the very same subject for the past twenty years. But until I read "Dianetics" it was simply a blind groping in total darkness. I agree with your theory in toto. Not having the background nor the scientific approach to tackle the problem I have been forced to confine myself to mere conjecture.

Although I have talked to many people who teach or preach science of mind, I have always run up against the wall of religion before I did even grasp the truth. I guess the number seven key is holding up the works. I am employed by the above firm and have been with them for the past eight years.

At the age of thirty-two I accepted a job as a delivery boy, in order to be able to get into the sacred portals of this make-believe world. Since then I have advanced to the important and highly paid position of construction clerk (my salary is seventy dollars per week). The goal I had hoped to reach long before this is as much out of sight now as it has ever been. Somehow I have never been able to carry out a single purpose to its conclusion.

Up until eight years ago I was a wanderer and ne'er-do-well. I have got into plenty of trouble during the past forty years, most of which has been of my own doing. Eight years ago I decided that I had better stop and take stock before I drowned in the sea of my own ignorance. So I got married and took the first steady job I have been able to hold on to for the first time in my life. My married life is not too good and I have not done too well in my work. Again the number seven key.

I have spent money I could ill afford on professional mind probing. I have many fears and complexes. I am always undecided about things. I make friends very rapidly and lose them the same way. I would have given up long ago were it not for one factor. I felt and still do that some day there would come a solution to all my problems, imaginary and real. When I read your article I knew that this was it.

A lot of the terms are a bit dense to me. And although I am going to purchase your book during my lunch hour today, I doubt that I will be able to apply much of it to myself. My education is nil (formal that is) and the only thing that saves me from being totally ignorant is the fact that I have been reading since the age of seven and traveling since the age of fourteen. I started with the complete works of Jules Verne and have kept up with science fiction ever since. Not only have I been reading the stuff because to me it is damn good literature but also because I knew that some day I would find something that would help me in my own life.

I am not suffering from delusions of grandeur nor do I claim to be the most ignorant individual in the city of Los Angeles. And every once in a while I get a bright glimmer of what life could be if man could only rid himself of his inhibitions or engrams.

By this time you have begun to wonder what the hell this letter is all about. Well it is simply this. You have mentioned that out of two hundred patients treated you have had two hundred complete cures. Now when I say that I too want to be cured, you are going to say, "So what" who the hell does this guy Dessler think he is, insisting that he wants to be cured.

Well I know that it is possible. Yoga has done nothing for me, neither has any of the science of mind stuff that is being peddled all over the country, particularly in Los Angeles. Your approach is the first one I have read that struck a responsive chord.

Please tell me what I can do to help myself first in order to be able to help others later. I am not interested in any possible fortune I may be able to make. I just want to find peace for once in my life. I want to be able to live with my fellow men without hate or scorn. I want to be able to repay my wife for all the effort she has made in my behalf. I want to be able to help others who are in the same hole I find myself in.

Please help me to rid myself of my personal demons and key number seven. How do I go about it and what do I do? I doubt if I can effect a self cure just by reading your book. I doubt that I shall be able to even understand it fully. But I do know that if two hundred patients were cured, I can be too. I am willing to do anything to achieve this. Even to quitting my unimportant little job. Because I know that once a cure is effected there shall be no problem of unemployment any longer.

You can't refuse me the chance to live, when I have often considered suicide as the only solution. I know that I shall hear from you. And until then I await your reply, if not with prayer, at least with hope.

Sincerely
Frank B. Dessler
404 N. Curson Ave.
Los Angeles 36, California

June 17, 1950

Mr. L. Ron Hubbard
42 Aberdeen Road
Elizabeth, New Jersey

My dear Mr. Hubbard:

We wish to respectfully call your attention to clause number 4 in the Lease which you have on premises located at the above address, which indicates that "Tenant shall use the premises hereby leased exclusively for a private residence (unless otherwise specified herein)."

The volume of cars parked in front of the property, and other conditions, indicates semi-business or professional use, which is prohibited. May we please ask you to refrain from creating any circumstances that would violate the terms of the Lease.

Very truly yours,
r. e. Scott co.
Otto Gabler

MR. GABLER—

HAPPILY FOR ME IF UNHAPPILY FOR YOU I HAVE A BOOK ON THE BESTSELLER LISTS. THE VOLUME OF TRAFFIC CANNOT BE STOPPED. I AM RENTING A LARGE NEW YORK OFFICE. THE LEASE, I WILL VACATE AS SOON AS I CAN FIND OTHER QUARTERS IF YOU SO DESIRE.

L. RON HUBBARD

Above Dictating answers to the mailbags of inquiring letters from readers

Left Ron's Elizabeth, New Jersey, home, where the first Dianetics Foundation was formed

To Mrs. Elizabeth Byall

Among others who made their way to the wilds of New Jersey in the wake of Dianetics were several troubled psychotherapists in search of a means to effectively treat neurosis. Most notable among them was Mrs. Elizabeth Byall. To what is recounted through the pages of her heartfelt letter from the summer of 1950, we might mention Mrs. Byall soon adopted Dianetics entirely and soon regained the use of her legs, numbed since a childhood bout with polio. ■

Mrs. Evan Bruce Byall

Quandary Hill, Gladwyne, Pennsylvania

Dear Mr. Hubbard:

Perhaps because my experience with you on Sunday made so profound an impression—perhaps because of what yesterday and today brought forth—tonight finds me in need of moral support.

My personal reaction to Sunday continues in almost the same "turned on" intensity in that I have been as disturbed ever since as I was at the time except that I have maintained a controlled exterior. I am certain you must have known that you reactivated much more than the events we covered all of which has left me in a state just slightly less than radioactive.

Yesterday was a witch of a day anyway and tackled with four hours' sleep so I finally cancelled all but one of my psychotherapy appointments, deliberately choosing the patient I thought the best for a first run. And I really hit the jackpot. There was one terrific hitch in that much of the content further reactivated *me* and I certainly was charmed that my patient couldn't see the tears her auditor was shedding part of the time! Today I ran this same patient through again and I can see I'm really in for it: she's solid engrams! I also did a trial run on my assistant who was one of my patient protégés. I knew she'd be a tough gal to tackle; a little over two years ago she terminated a seven-year psycho-neurosis-depression by nearly going overboard and a half-hearted suicide attempt. Needless to say she has been through plenty—plenty of hell and plenty of therapy. But could be you'd have been a little proud of me; I got through!

We are all so genuinely excited, Mr. Hubbard, and so eager to work with this approach on so many people who need it so desperately!

If it is still extant, and Dear God I hope it is! I want to accept your invitation to see you in New York. I am not just certain when you said you would be there. I'm afraid I wish it could be right away or else that we had brought you home with us! My psyche always gives me hell anyway and now between what you activated on Sunday and the terrific ride I am aware I have been taking recently in my much-increased patient load in psychotherapy—well, I'm having something of a rugged time.

Left After outgrowing Ron's home on Aberdeen Road, the Dianetics Foundation moved to the Miller Building, 275 Morris Avenue, Elizabeth, New Jersey

I enclose, because you may be interested, my article from the May Journal. Of course it has been edited and is but a vestigial remain of the original.

I wait to hear you say I am still invited.

Most sincerely,
Elizabeth Byall

Tuesday, June twenty-seventh

Elizabeth Byall

July 3, 1950

Mrs. Elizabeth Byall
Quandary Hill
Gladwyne, Pennsylvania

Dear Mrs. Byall:

I enjoyed reading your article very much, but even more, your letter. Thank you very much for sending them to me.

We will have two offices—one at 275 Morris Avenue, Elizabeth, New Jersey, where Administration will be done, and one at 55 East 82nd Street, New York City, where training and therapy will be done. We will not be in New York for another ten or twelve days. Until that time, I can be reached here in Elizabeth. Information will have our 'phone number.

It may be of interest to you to know that the chief of research of the Block Chemical Company has been undergoing Dianetic therapy. His spine was terribly deformed by a polio attack when he was a small child, and after a few weeks of therapy he has grown one inch and from all indications should experience a gratifying recovery. It is his opinion on research that polio is to a marked degree psychosomatic.

I hope to see you again and be assured that within the limits imposed upon me, my time is at your disposal.

My very best regards,
L. Ron Hubbard

July 24 '50

Dear Mr. Hubbard,

Here is a question about an *apparently* recovered case of post-traumatic epilepsy. The case is myself—male, white, 24.

Since you did not mention the possible complications of brain scars or the extent to which they might require professional treatment, I feel compelled to broach the question. During the attacks, which lasted from June of 1938 to June of 1940, I must have acquired a fine mess of engrams, as many of the attacks were in public.

The attacks occurred about every three weeks, at one time reaching 75 days (I always counted) and near the end the intervals were only about seven to ten days. On June 21, 1940 I had seventeen attacks and on July 1, I went to Mayo's, still ignorant of the trouble. It was diagnosed as a "scar on the brain." Phenobarbital and Dilantin were prescribed. Since then I have had no attacks, though I have been frightened by apparent returns of the "aura," which was always particularly vivid, mystic and long-drawn-out. For instance, something in the coda of the first movement of the Beethoven Ninth once triggered an aura in me, though I became interested in music two years after the last attack. I have almost ceased to use either drug, but have noticed no connection between non-use and return of the aura.

None of my personality troubles can be traced to any physical derangement at the moment, but I am rather afraid that any attempts at Dianetic treatment may cause a return to some of the moments of the attacks. As a matter of fact, there is a faint possibility that the (I hope) pseudo-auras may be caused by engramic factors.

Now, is it safe, unsafe or have you thought about the subject? Should I get a doctor to perform the therapy, which I so badly need that I cannot hold a job, or should I just go along? Here I am, expecting for my wife to have a baby in a little over two months and no job. At times I am a pretty good writer, but not good enough to finish a story satisfactorily, though pretty good on short poems and articles about music. I am supposed to be a walking encyclopedia, but my memories and usefulness are no good to me to make money.

These are personality troubles, probably curable, but I simply wanted to show you that I am not a case in which the epilepsy has begun to deteriorate the mind (another "I hope").

Incidentally, I met a boy who said that he remembered that I was hit on the head with a baseball bat a few weeks before the attacks started, so there will probably be no prenatal worry about that particular trauma. Also, the first time that I heard it called epilepsy was when I was examined for military service. Then the examining doctor grandly wrote it out. All of the doctors around had been so apathetic on the subject that when I came back from Mayo's, we sent reports on my progress back to Doctor McNiell by way of a friend who went every year. That was the reason why the ugly word had never come up before.

Maybe this will rate a personal reply, as I have seen no group answer in ASF and have read your book through twice.

Thank You
John Daves Roberts
Box 84, Choccolocco, Alabama

$$\Longleftarrow\!\!\gtrless\!\!\gtrless\!\!\gtrless\!\!\Longrightarrow$$

July 29, 1950

Mr. John Daves Roberts
Box 84
Choccolocco, Alabama

My dear Mr. Roberts:

There is a small amount of misinformation in your letter. Although it has been popularly believed that in insanity and nervous disorders, there was nerve scar or deterioration, no evidence to date has confirmed it, and those people who were apparently suffering from nervous scarring have recovered beautifully.

There is very little data available on epilepsy at this time, however, several cases have been run and no recurrence of attacks or deterioration of the case has been evidenced. If it is true that you were hit on the head before the attacks started; that blow was probably a key-in to prenatal incidents. If you can remember the incident yourself, of being hit on the head, it will probably key-out the attacks, if that was the beginning of your trouble.

We have no one at this time in Alabama who might be considered an expert auditor, but I am sure an intelligent friend, after a very thorough study of the manual and adhering strictly to its rules and particularly to the Auditor's Code, should be able to make progress in your case. If you have a doctor available who is willing to use Dianetics and who has time to study it, then certainly use him.

I am not advocating that you begin Dianetic processing nor am I prescribing for your epilepsy. If that is what the condition is, I am only giving you a general opinion as to the abilities of Dianetics.

Please let us hear from you again.

Sincerely yours,
L. Ron Hubbard

Aug. 15, 1950

Norman W. James
1736½ Richmond Rd.
Houston 6, Texas

Dear Mr. Hubbard:

After 184 hours' work with Dianetics, I can only say that I have become more and more convinced of its basic value every hour I have worked with it.

I have seen it work on two of my close friends, one an engineer and the other a musician and writer. They were both quite sane to begin with, but now they have a mental stability and happiness *far* greater than the average person. The energy and optimism that they now have is above and beyond anything I ever witnessed before Dianetics.

Another recommendation for Dianetics is that the more intelligent people accept it more quickly than others. When I tell them that I have personally seen most of the statements made in the book, Dianetics, proven in my own living room. And that *anyone* who is willing to read the book carefully can, in the same manner, prove it for himself. They usually get the book and read it.

When Dianetics is accepted (as it inevitably will be accepted) it will by itself bring on a golden age. A world of happiness, peace, and prosperity!

Sincerely yours,
Norman W. James

Norman James

716 Broadway,
San Diego 1, California.
November 27, 1950

Mr. L. Ron Hubbard
Box 502,
Elizabeth, N. J.

Dear Ron:

This salutation seems on the presumptuous side when it has been twelve years since I saw you last.

You may remember something of my background, though our contacts were few and too brief. For nearly eight years I made my living as a psychologist, stumbled onto a means of temporarily overcoming some of the worst effects of aberrations and such, and lectured some in India in 1935–6. For seven years I operated the San Francisco Fiction School and broadcast The Fiction Forum.

Your discoveries are a revelation, a down-to-earth revelation, to one who knows something of the mind and mental processes. You have possibly opened the way to a racial cosmic consciousness. At the least, yours is the greatest single contribution to the welfare and advancement of the human man. (How's that for authority?)

I have read your book. My wife and I are beginning therapy. What can we do to further the cause? What do you consider most important at this stage?

My view, though narrow at this time, is that a nationwide introduction to Dianetics is the first step. This is being done through the wide sale of your book, but inasmuch as all people won't read it and some won't understand it a lecture program is indicated. Also I have been day-dreaming of the effect of "clearing" a chosen city. This would be an example and unassailable proof of Dianetics.

May we not hear from you?

Yours,
Wilford J. Rasmussen

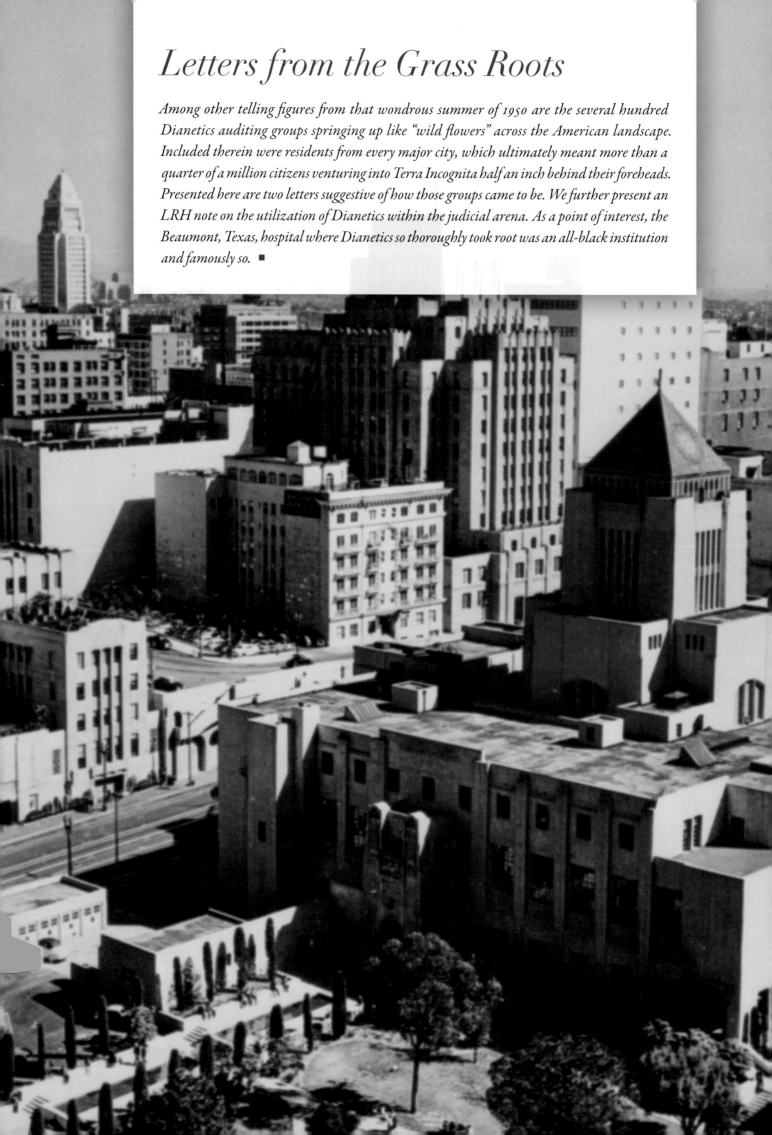

Letters from the Grass Roots

Among other telling figures from that wondrous summer of 1950 are the several hundred Dianetics auditing groups springing up like "wild flowers" across the American landscape. Included therein were residents from every major city, which ultimately meant more than a quarter of a million citizens venturing into Terra Incognita half an inch behind their foreheads. Presented here are two letters suggestive of how those groups came to be. We further present an LRH note on the utilization of Dianetics within the judicial arena. As a point of interest, the Beaumont, Texas, hospital where Dianetics so thoroughly took root was an all-black institution and famously so. ■

DOUGLAS HOSPITAL CLINIC
MODERN ★ THOROUGHLY EQUIPPED
935 BUFORD STREET – PHONE 4787
BEAUMONT, TEXAS

July 22, 1950

The Hubbard Dianetic Research Foundation
P.O. Box 502
Elizabeth, N. J.

Dear Sirs:

Enclosed you will find check for $15.00 for associate membership. Not because of taking the financially most economically considered way, even though I see nothing wrong with that thought, but because it is the most practical solution to my problem relative to Dianetics. I have views concerning financial support of the institution in this section and you are aware that results have bountiful financial rewards.

I am a licensed physician and surgeon operating a registered privately owned and operated hospital (general hospital) covering the entire field of medical practice including general medicine, surgery, physical medicine—practically every mode of physical medicine we have found to be practical and productive of predictable results—and have been searching all of my aware life for something missing in medicine. We have always been practical in our institution. We accept nothing that won't compute, regardless to whether it came from the Mayo Clinic, Johns Hopkins, Ochsner Clinic, postgraduate courses in medicine and surgery, or from some little hamlet or village or some obscure individual. This missing element always eluded us.

Our routine is to practice standard medicine first. If it works, fine. If not, you must take another step. *Still something was missing.* We knew the missing element dwelled in the field we understood as psychiatry at the time but still we couldn't compute it and didn't nor couldn't compute our inability to understand into the unsolved equation.

SINCE OUR EXPERIENCE WITH DIANETICS, MANY COMPUTABLE POSTULATES KEEP BOUNCING UP INTO OUR MINDS CONCERNING THESE FACTS. These postulates are glaringly obvious. You can see them now without having your attention called to them. It seems that the missing elements now are merely tied in with the obvious postulates that DIANETICS has made possible to be uncovered.

I am omitting much detail because I know you are too busy to be bothered. I am only a preclear. My wife and I are auditing each other. I am very impatient with her even though I am thoroughly aware of the fact that she is doing the very best she can.

She was violently against Dianetics in the beginning because she considered it as a reflection on her intelligence to assume that she needed mental therapy and further cited the fact that I never believed anything under the sun that couldn't be proven as proof of the fact that I was abnormal and obviously the one in the greatest need of therapy. I cannot argue against facts and she had facts. However, now, she is just as enthusiastic about DIANETICS as I am. She censures herself for her slowness in progressive understanding of DIANETICS. (Thank goodness she isn't aware of the fact that she should be censuring her auditor—but I am terrifically busy and her file clerk knows his business and I do wish he would soon bring up the engram that makes her think that any scientific treatise is automatically difficult to understand), however I do hope when we go to Los Angeles in August for vacation I will be able to aid her—with more available time—to understand the entire handbook on DIANETICS. With a little help, she will make an excellent auditor.

We have four other members on the hospital staff that we will make auditors out of as soon as we return from the West Coast. It is my intention to have no employee in this hospital who isn't at least a release. Our key personnel must be Clears. That has become axiomatic with me because it is unquestionably obvious as to the benefits to us and the public and the understandings of the mechanisms involved in operating room conversation. We have been guilty of too much talking in the operating room. Our visiting staff physicians will apparently be the hardest nuts to crack about conversation around anesthetized patients and semi and comatose patients. THERE IS NO END TO THE CHANGES DIANETICS IS BRINGING ABOUT IN OUR HOSPITAL. Much calculates in the needs of understanding and conduct of hospital employees and staff as well as physical arrangements and isolation techniques necessary for post anesthetic cases and other unaware individuals.

Trust you will forgive me for this long dissertation. I do wish to be associated, as an associate member—(preferably a full-fledged member but I cannot spare the time)—of the Hubbard Dianetic Research Foundation.*

Yours truly,
J. S. Douglas, M.D.

A Doctor Holiday of the Douglas Hospital Clinic was trained at the Los Angeles Hubbard Dianetic Research Foundation shortly after the drafting of this letter. He then returned to Beaumont to oversee the training of all hospital staff in the application of Dianetics, very much including Dr. Douglas.

Tampa Business College
FOUNDED 1890

FREE GRADUATE PLACEMENT SERVICE

104 N. EDISON AT GRAND CENTRAL
TAMPA 6, FLORIDA

September 9, 1950

The Hubbard Dianetic Research Foundation
P.O. Box 502
Elizabeth, N. J.

Gentlemen:

In March of 1940, I awakened one morning to find that the entire visual field of my left eye was clouded and I could not distinguish shapes or forms with it but only saw dark blurs, as through a thick fog. My doctor had me admitted to the hospital with a diagnosis of acute uveitis, and after a month, during which both eyes were kept continuously dilated, and a tonsillectomy was performed (in an effort to remove a "focus of infection") I was released and able to return to my work, but compelled to use strong glasses. While my left eye was never again completely clouded, on the average of once or twice a month I would spend a few days of extreme discomfort with spots, halo effects, and painful internal ocular pressure. This usually occurred anytime I had been doing work that placed a strain on my eyes, or had contracted a cold, or otherwise had lowered resistance.

I was first audited in June of this year by Lyman Budlong, 120 S. Fremont Avenue, Tampa, Florida, and in my first session reduced a prenatal engram containing a severe somatic in the left eye. It however proved to be but one engram of a very long chain—for each session after that, we contacted a similar engram with an eye somatic. After about 15 hours of processing, some peculiar things began happening. I had continued wearing my glasses, but students, teachers, and other workers in this College began noticing that when I had a letter or memorandum to read, or found it necessary to look at something closely, I *unconsciously* reached up, not to adjust my glasses, but to lift them entirely away from and above my eyes, in order to see more clearly! This continued for two or three days, I am told, until finally someone couldn't resist the temptation to call my attention to it, and then a little experimenting made me aware of the fact that I could see much better without my glasses than I could with them.

Frankly, this surprised me! My interest in Dianetics had not been associated with this visual impairment (I had not given any thought to the possibility) but solely because of a desire to gain a better understanding of the human mind. At the suggestion of several members of the Tampa Bay Dianetic Research Institute, and to satisfy my own curiosity, I visited Dr. L. L. Fernandez, an optometrist of this city, and requested that he make complete tests of my vision. He did so and reported to me that my vision was perfect and that only very faintly perceptible scars were left of the old uvea infection (he said that if he had not known they were supposed to be there, he would not have seen them).

In addition to this benefit, there was another which I personally consider more significant. For the last three years my general physical tone had been so poor that I remained under the constant treatment of Dr. G. E. Day, 508 South Willow Avenue, of this city, for anemia and low blood pressure. During this entire time, my blood pressure had hovered between 80 and 85 over 40 to 50; I suffered from general neurasthenia, and probably was on the verge of entering the rapidly descending spiral. My pulse was usually somewhere around 98 to 100. But, by August of this year, all this had changed. My blood pressure came up to 108 during the first week of August and was up to 120 by the end of the month (almost optimum for my age and type, I was told). My pulse had dropped to normal. For three years I had taken bottles of folic acid, vitamin pills, adhered strictly to "build-up" diets, received liver extract injections, etc., but with no apparent results. To Dianetic techniques do I give full credit for this release. Incidentally, the engramic content that seemed responsible for much of this, were statements like "I'm numb all over, my whole body seems dead," uttered by my mother during an illness prior to my birth.

My doctor was so impressed by this rise up the Tone Scale that he obtained a copy of the handbook and began using Dianetics in his practice.

It is our hope that we did not act prematurely or in conflict with the programs being planned by the Foundation when we organized the Tampa Bay Dianetic Research Institute, including members from Tampa, St. Petersburg, Clearwater, and other surrounding towns, and began functioning as an information and coordinating center. Associate Membership in this Institute is open to all interested in Dianetics. Full membership is limited to those who have obtained releases, and who desire to do auditing and take part in the research program of the Institute.

A branch of the Tampa Bay Dianetic Research Institute has been established at the University of Florida, in Gainesville, and correspondence may be addressed to their acting secretary, Mr. Frank Smith, Box 2611, University Station, Gainesville, Florida. In your previous letter, mention was made of an active group in Miami. We would appreciate being supplied with their address in order that we may refer to them interested individuals from that city and vicinity who contact the Tampa group. One of our members has recently opened offices for the practice of medicine in that city and is very desirous of affiliating with the Miami group.

Very sincerely,
Morgan J. Morey, Dean
TAMPA BUSINESS COLLEGE

A. V. FALCONE

SUITE 1018 PERSHING SQUARE BUILDING

448 SOUTH HILL STREET

LOS ANGELES 13

MADISON 9-3101

December 8, 1950

Mr. L. Ron Hubbard

2600 S. Hoover

Los Angeles, California

Dear Mr. Hubbard:

I heard your talk last Sunday at the Guild Theatre.

I was greatly impressed by the tremendous potential of Dianetics, if properly "handled," in the social sciences. Its particular application to the fields of political science and sociology is so patently timely that I feel your greatest emphasis should be made in that direction.

With best wishes, I am

Sincerely,

A. V. Falcone

—————————————————◇◇◇◇◇◇◇◇————————————————

2600 S. Hoover Street

Los Angeles 7, Calif.

December 27, 1950

Dear Mr. Falcone:

Thank you very much for your note of December 8 about the Guild Theatre talk.

The highest goal of Dianetics is the auditing of groups in an effort to better human relations not only in corporations and companies but in nations. The compilation of basic axioms for this purpose has been in progress for a long while and is just now culminating, and workable techniques and pilot projects are now being run.

It may additionally interest you that I have a report here that the Committee on Evidence of the New York Bar Association is tremendously interested in Dianetics since in Judiciary Dianetics certain tenets are advanced which, according to their statement, antiquate many current rules of evidence. They are reported to be undertaking a considerable study of this subject.

Thank you again for your interest. With my very best regards,

Yours sincerely,

L. Ron Hubbard

Right Auditing demonstration,
Los Angeles, 1950

Concerning Asia

Although otherwise self-explanatory, we might provide two ancillary notes on those letters pertaining to the introduction of Dianetics to a then still devastated Japan. In the first place, Ron had spent much of his youth in the Orient and, actually, spoke some Japanese—hence, his remark, "I am not unacquainted with the various patterns of language which would lie in a Japanese reactive mind." In the second place, he would long describe the taking of Japanese lives in combat as his one regrettable act. ■

4527 Westway Place
Dallas, Texas
June 19, 1950

Dear Mr. Hubbard:

At the end of May I mailed a copy of your new book *Dianetics* to Dr. Kisaburo Kawabe, the Sociology Professor of Komazawa University, and suggested that he contact you about the possibility of translating your work into Japanese, since I was very deeply impressed with it myself. My friend Mr. Alvin Jett reviewed the book for the *Dallas Morning News* and caused me to buy a copy in the first place; he was also good enough to try out Dianetics on me and, while he has now gone north for vacation after a few brief sessions, we were both dumbfounded by the accuracy of your theories in practice as proved in the few hours we were able to devote to it.

I speak and write Japanese and would be very glad to help Dr. Kawabe of Komazawa with his translation of *Dianetics,* if you should decide to give him the translation rights. I think he is a wise and good man in all probability.

I imagine the appearance of your book must have brought you hundreds of letters like this one. Even the briefest note on a practicing Dianeticist in Dallas and on your opinion of Kawabe as translator would be deeply appreciated.

Yours respectfully,
Sam Houston Brock, Jr.

June 23, 1950

Mr. Sam Houston Brock, Jr.
4527 Westway Place
Dallas, Texas

My dear Mr. Brock:

I saw the publisher of Dianetics this afternoon, Mr. Art Ceppos, who had to hand a letter from Dr. Kisaburo Kawabe relative to the translation of Dianetics into Japanese. It was the opinion of Mr. Ceppos that an equitable arrangement could be made on the book with a full understanding of the price and publication difficulties existing in Japan.

About two years ago I did some speculation about the possible effect of Dianetics upon Japan and surmised that if Dianetics were to be imported and sturdily promulgated there the effects of her defeat could rather easily be overcome and she could be rehabilitated through Dianetics by her own efforts into a first class power once more, possessed perhaps of better skill and direction which would permit her to avoid some of the pitfalls into which her recent course led her. Out of duty to my country, but through no dislike of the Japanese whom I have all my life greatly admired and respected, I was forced to share a part in the events leading to her recent defeat. Not because my own war efforts were destructive to her, but because they are upon my conscience I am glad if my work, which after all belongs to all men, can aid her spirit and prosperity.

I am not unacquainted with the various patterns of language which would lie in a Japanese reactive mind. The homonymic character of the tongue and its lack of articles and pronouns might render it very forceful in engramic commands. Having visited the islands of Japan in my youth and numbering amongst my friends many able Japanese, it has been my conviction for the past twenty-three years that the Orient was in great need of the intellect, cleanliness and ability of the Japanese. And it was with grief that I beheld her extending a conquest by force which inevitably would have come about in due time from superiority alone, and would have pervaded Asia to its great benefit without the destruction attendant upon the precipitancy of war.

It is my belief that the Orient needs Japan and that Japan could yet elevate herself to a point of cultural superiority so forceful that the only true conquest, the conquest by ideas, creativeness and construction could be effected throughout Asia, and that Japan is the single and only hope of a blood-stained East. It would be an ample and adequate reward for those labors I have expended should Dianetics prove to be a stepping-stone upon the road to Japan's establishment of herself as the arbiter of Asian destiny.

Peace, to any man of action, is a stupid and antipathetic thing since it connotes a dreary and unchanged monotony and a contented and sinking stagnation. It was through combat and his taste for conflict that brought man from the mire of swamps and set him as the king of earth. And those who talk of peace talk without knowledge of the inherent necessity for action within men. Combat and conflict, however, become undesirable when expressed in terms of man at war with men. There are far too many targets for man's combative energies for him to indulge the social aberration called war. Conflict with other life forms such as bacteria, conflict between man and space, man and time, man and aberration, bring about desirable gains in man's ability to persevere in his survival. Overcoming the natural enemies of man and conquering them so that they then align their forces with man to further such natural conquests, is the combat force direction which has brought man to the elevation he now enjoys. And a further practice of such principles cannot but raise man to nearly indestructible heights. Thus one can see that Japan's conquest of herself and through her heightened conquest Asia is not only feasible but desirable to the best interests of mankind as a whole. Her most effective mission would be to restore to their own destiny the aberrated and oppressed peoples of Asian lands. And this might best be done by arming them with knowledges and culture sufficient to maintain them in a greatly enhanced environment. Along such a course lies greatness, a greatness unsullied by the filth and disgrace of human war.

These things I write to you because I know that you will soon be in Japan. Should you wish to communicate my sentiments with regard to that Nation in any way you are perfectly free to do so. As an American you could not misconstrue my

"Dianetics"

sentiments with regard to Asia. I consider China to be in a state of hopeless confusion and political delusion, differing not greatly from the yesterdays when I knew her gripped by senseless internal convulsions, oppressed by disease, starvation and lack of engineering. The loss of Japanese influence in the Orient is already responsible for much of the Asian confusion, just as the precipitation of Japan's war lords made it possible for Russia to despoil the nation we had defeated. I am taking no political stand beyond the blunt statement that I believe in freedom for mankind in its most thoroughly extended sense and believe further that this freedom is unattainable so long as man staggers under the crushing burden of social aberrations. A defeated Japan and a crazed China are poor risks to the health of mankind at large.

Your own efforts in helping Doctor Kawabe are not only desirable, but would probably be vitally necessary since such a translation would require a colloquial knowledge of English on the one hand and a knowledge of colloquial Japanese on the other. Further, you express here a good fundamental understanding of Dianetic techniques without which no translator could accomplish a useful translation. I shall make it my business to forward to you or to Doctor Kawabe, Foundation bulletins as soon as they are published. These contain much information and techniques more fully developed than those expressed in the present handbook. By including them in the Japanese translation these bulletins would make the Japanese edition much more up to date than the currently existing handbook. Dianetics travels very swiftly in its advance and few days pass without something new being added to its repertoire.

Should you aid in the Japanese promulgation of Dianetics you may find yourself swept up in its impetus there. Avalanches of letters tell us that it is running like wildfire through the United States. Should you become interested in the Dianetic aspect in Japan upon the assurance of your abilities there, it may be possible for us to create a Japanese department of the Foundation in Japan. Such a step might easily be financed by the book royalties accruing from its publication there, and would give Dianetics and the world the benefit of the intelligent and careful work for which Japanese scientists are famous.

I have answered you at length about your Japanese venture and voyage but I can give you very little in the way of advice as to auditors in Dallas. We are making auditors as swiftly as we can but it will be a long time before very many professionals are available. I have, however, in the files one name from Dallas. I do not know anything about this gentleman beyond the fact that he sent us a letter. However, it may help you to give you his name, which is John W. Sarber, P. O. Box 7062, Dallas, Texas.

Hoping to hear from you again and with very best wishes for a pleasant voyage.

Best regards,
L. Ron Hubbard

Right Japanese edition of *Dianetics: The Modern Science of Mental Health* as published today

クリアー

ダイアネティックスでは、最適の状態にある人間を「クリアー」と呼びます。この言葉は名詞として、また動詞として、本書の中に繰り返し出てきます。そこでまず初めに、ダイアネティックス療法の目標であるクリアーとはどのようなものかを正確に説明しておきましょう。

クリアーを調べ、あらゆる精神病、ノイローゼ、強迫観念、抑圧など（どれも逸脱）の有無、また心因性の病気と呼ばれる自己発生的な病気の有無について見てみましょう。テストの結果からはっきりわかることは、クリアーにはそうした病気や逸脱が全く見られないということです。さらに知能検査の結果から、クリアーの知能は平均よりも高いことがわかります。行動面を観察してみると、活気に溢れた、満足の行く生き方を追求していることがわかります。

一方、これらのテスト結果は、比較によっても得られます。ノイローゼで心因性の病気を持っている人に同様のテストを行うと、逸脱や病気を持っていることがわかります。そこで、こうしたノイローゼや病気をクリアリングによって完全に取り除いていくために、ダイアネティックス療法を用います。最終的には、前述したクリアーと同じテスト結果が得られるでしょう。ちなみに、この実験は何度も行われ、常に結果は一定でした。神経

13

From a Student at the First Foundation

Providing yet another view from the eye of that Dianetics storm through the summer of 1950 is the somewhat chatty letter from a student of the first Professional Auditor's Course at Elizabeth, New Jersey. In addition to a fascinating comment on the first Dianetic Clears, one might consider the reference to Ron's much anticipated appearance in California. Contrary to what is suggested here, however, the Founder of Dianetics did indeed provide professional training to students of the Los Angeles Foundation. ■

Hotel Park East
1065 East Jersey St
Elizabeth 4, N. J.
7/8/50

Dear Charlie:

You said you wanted any printed new dope as fast as it came out—on Dianetics I mean. Well there just hasn't been any—that is—in print. That stuff Brad Shank got over the phone and mimeographed in LA is not exactly correct. I've never seen a copy of it but hear by grapevine that Hubbard disapproved of it. The reason nothing has come out in print for general distribution yet (even to us in the professional course) is they've been too busy with the tremendous volume of mail, and phone calls from *all* over the country, training auditors and finding a place to operate in.

When the book was published Ron never dreamed of this kind of response. He never intended (originally) an auditors course and Foundation as now exists. But the response forced him to get together with John Campbell, Dr. Winter, Don Rogers, Parker Morgan and Art Ceppos and form a Foundation. I've met them all—all nice guys. However haven't been able to get next—or very close—to John Campbell. He seems cold and uncordial. I think he's going through a restimulation almost constantly.

Anyway they were going to buy a large estate to house the Foundation but some psychiatric sanitarium nearby objected and got neighbors to put pressure on etc. so no deal. In the meantime mail and phone calls coming in but fast. So the whole thing moved into Ron's house—a large one in a very nice residential district. But it became too small and also neighbors complained—cars in streets etc. so he was evicted and just this week we all moved to the whole 4th floor of the Miller Bldg 275 Morris Ave Elizabeth. In addition Ron is busy with all sorts of misc biz such as acquiring a house in NY for NY branch. The prof course may move there July 15.

Anyway they have *not* put out anything other than the form letter enclosed.

However, there's oodles of new stuff Ron gives out in lectures. I have recordings of most of it. A few new wrinkles I think of now that I *know* are not in book:

1) No need to count people into reverie anymore—just have them close their eyes.

2) Basic-basic is now considered to be the sperm sequence.

3) Self-control mechanism in the form of demon circuit is most difficult of cases. That's you, Van and me. By the way I find I don't have Van's address here so will you please share this entire letter with Van—and give him and Mayne my best.

Left Students of the first Dianetics Foundation, Elizabeth, New Jersey, 1950

There are hundreds more new things—some big some little—I can't remember them offhand but would be glad to answer (or get the answer) for any question you or Van may have on *any* phase of the subject.

In exchange for this I'd appreciate it extremely if you would please give me something of a report on what is happening in LA on the following fronts: Dianetics, Roundtable, Coord. Council (did you get the check?) and general gossip. But most important of all what's doing with Watkins and the course in Dianetic Auditing I'm planning to give.

Incidentally, before I forget it I want to here and now offer both you (and Van too if he wants) a free course if you care to attend. Keep this under your hats though. I'm quite sure Hubbard will *not* offer a course when he comes to LA. Also feel I've sold him on talking to the Roundtable—will know more definitely later.

As to the course here we start Monday (July 10) with a 2½ hr lecture at 8 AM every day (instead of at noon as previously). Then following that we audit each other, watch others audit and are watched in our auditing by more experienced auditors.

My therapy is a little hard getting started. I've had 19½ hrs so far and no basic-basic though plenty of boil-off in basic area.

It seems a Clear wants to keep it a secret till there are more like him so he won't be such a curiosity piece and be tested to death etc.

Later 7/11

Here is the *first* thing off the press—it is just out today and was done by one of the students here. I'm getting some pretty good recordings. At least I hope they're all good. Haven't had the time to listen to all of them back. Well Chas, let me hear from you. Regards to Marie.

Sincerely
Andy.

The Hubbard Dianetic Research Foundation
P. O. BOX 502, ELIZABETH, N. J.
ELizabeth 3-2951

THE HUBBARD DIANETIC RESEARCH FOUNDATION

ANNOUNCES THE OPENING OF THE

Los Angeles Department

TUESDAY, AUGUST 15, 1950

A professional course of one month's duration will be taught personally by L. Ron Hubbard. For course reservations and therapy, write P. O. Box 14,551, Los Angeles 4, Calif.

Open Letters from the First Foundations

Although nominally posted on the first Foundation boards and possessing no real legal say as to the administration of those Foundations, Ron nonetheless had much to say on how those organizations should not be administered: "Dianetics has succeeded almost in direct ratio to the amount of service it has delivered to the public and in inverse ratio to the efforts the Foundations have made to make money." Reflective of such sentiments and more are his open letters to students and staff of the New Jersey and Los Angeles Dianetic Research Foundations. ■

THE FOUNDATION AS A PUBLIC SERVICE UNIT
22 November 1950

In the beginning, it was a necessary part of Foundation operations to finance itself so that it could carry forward Dianetics as an organization rather than as an individual.

Dianetics is a fully American development. As a part of that tradition, it has retained its independence of character and has had a self-supporting nature. The first difficulties had to do with the procurement and training of personnel. This initial obstacle has been overcome and there now exists sufficient personnel to form nucleus training and treatment units in important places.

Few people realize the magnitude of Dianetics or the demand which is placed upon the Foundation for service in terms of letters, free speakers, advices for charity cases. The Foundation has tried to answer these needs as it could.

We need many things because America needs many things. The reason why Dianetics has been so successful is because it answers a need which has not been filled in America—the successful treatment of any and all aberrations and psychosomatic illness. Until such time as more states and the federal government see fit to subsidize the Foundation properly, until such time as endowments from such organizations as the Ford Foundation are made available to the Dianetics Foundation, contributions from private citizens and the financial structure of the Foundation itself must carry the brunt. This is no small responsibility.

Rapt attention at an LRH lecture in Los Angeles, 1950

The casual observer may have thought to find in the early days of the Foundation a certain commercialism. An investigation of the books of the Foundation will demonstrate that funds received by the Foundation have been expended to the best of the Foundation's ability. That ability, for lack of administration and solid organization in the beginning, was not large. We have made our funds go as far as we could make them go.

We have the specific goals of emptying sanitariums and prisons and raising the general tone of the nation by the end of 1951. Without Dianetics, to dream of such a thing would have been foolhardy. With Dianetics, it is not only possible, it is already under accomplishment. In the Foundations, the staffs work from twelve to eighteen hours a day to make these dreams come true. We are giving all the help we can. We need all the help we can get.

L. Ron Hubbard

Left Los Angeles Foundation entrance
on 2600 South Hoover

ORGANIZATIONAL MEMORANDUM

27 November 1950

FROM: L. Ron Hubbard

TO: DIANETICS

SUBJECT: EXPANSION

1. It is one of the goals of Dianetics to become a public service organization, working with minimal cost to anyone. As soon as government and individual subsidy and book sales permit this, we will find the Foundations expanding even more rapidly. Patterns of operation are being created, tested and proven constantly. A stability of organization is desirable, but our stability for years to come will come only along the lines of stable expansion. It is on this basis that our organization should be laid: that only erratic changes can cause confusion and that planned expansion means smooth operation and stability.

2. The most valuable possession of Dianetics is its personnel, their skills, initiative, backgrounds and personal courage. We have to use our best personnel where they are and cannot promote them until they have replacement. The promotion of personnel is inherent in orderly expansion. To resolve this problem, it is requested that everyone in Dianetics find, within or without the organization, a replacement for himself and train that replacement into the details of his own job against a time—all too near—when promotion vacates the post. It is true that some promotion will not be possible for lack of replacement. None of us like disorder. Smooth operation comes from foresight. Train the best person you can find to hold the job you are holding. Don't get pinned down by either choosing and training an unable person or by finding and training none.

    Administration will act, within thirty days from this date, on the assumption that anyone to be promoted or shifted has left in his place a person fully qualified and trained to do that job. Chaos itself will reign if action is taken on an assumption for which there is no ground.

L. Ron Hubbard

Right Another typically packed Los Angeles lecture in December 1950

1951 JAN 15 PM 3

HUBBARD DIANETICS

275 MORRIS AVE ELIZABETH NJ

A FEW WEEKS AGO I WENT TO KANSAS CITY TO FIND OUT WHAT DIANETICS NEEDED
IN THE FIELD. I FOUND OUT SHOCKINGLY FAST. THEY NEEDED VALIDATION
MATERIAL AND A FAR SIMPLER COMMUNICATION OF TECHNIQUE SO I HAVE
SPEEDED UP THE VALIDATION PROGRAM SO PEOPLE CAN HAVE EVIDENCE AND
YOU NOW HAVE PRELIMINARY PAMPHLET WITH LOADS MORE PROOF TO FOLLOW. I
DESIGNED A NEW BOOK WITH NEW TECHNIQUES SO SIMPLE A KID CAN PRODUCE
CLEARS. I AM DEEP INTO THE WRITING OF THIS NEW BOOK. I WANT IT TO
GET TO PEOPLE SWIFTLY. BOOK CONTAINS THREE NEW FAST SIMPLE METHODS
OF KNOCKING OUT ENGRAMS. ONE OF THEM WILL CLEAR A PERSON OF ALL
MAJOR LOCKS IN TWENTY FIVE HOURS. IT CAN ENTIRELY KNOCK OUT ALL BAD
AUDITING A CASE HAS HAD IN TWO HOURS. ANOTHER WILL START INACCESSIBLE
OR LOW REALITY CASES SWIFTLY. A YEAR OF STUDY OF WHAT PEOPLE DID
WITH DIANETICS IS GOING INTO THE WRITING OF "DIANETICS: SCIENCE OF
SURVIVAL SIMPLIFIED TECHNIQUES." NOW THE SUBJECT CAN REALLY ROLL.
FIGURE OUT A METHOD OF RELEASING THIS MATERIAL PRE PUBLICATION. IT
MAY BE EXPENSIVE TO US BUT PEOPLE NEED IT. OFFER A PHOTO LITHO OF THE
ORIGINAL MANUSCRIPT REGARDLESS OF EXPENSE. YOU'VE GOT TO GET THIS
MATERIAL TO PEOPLE QUICK.

BEST REGARDS

RON

Music Hall in Kansas
City, Missouri, where
L. Ron Hubbard lectured
in the fall of 1950

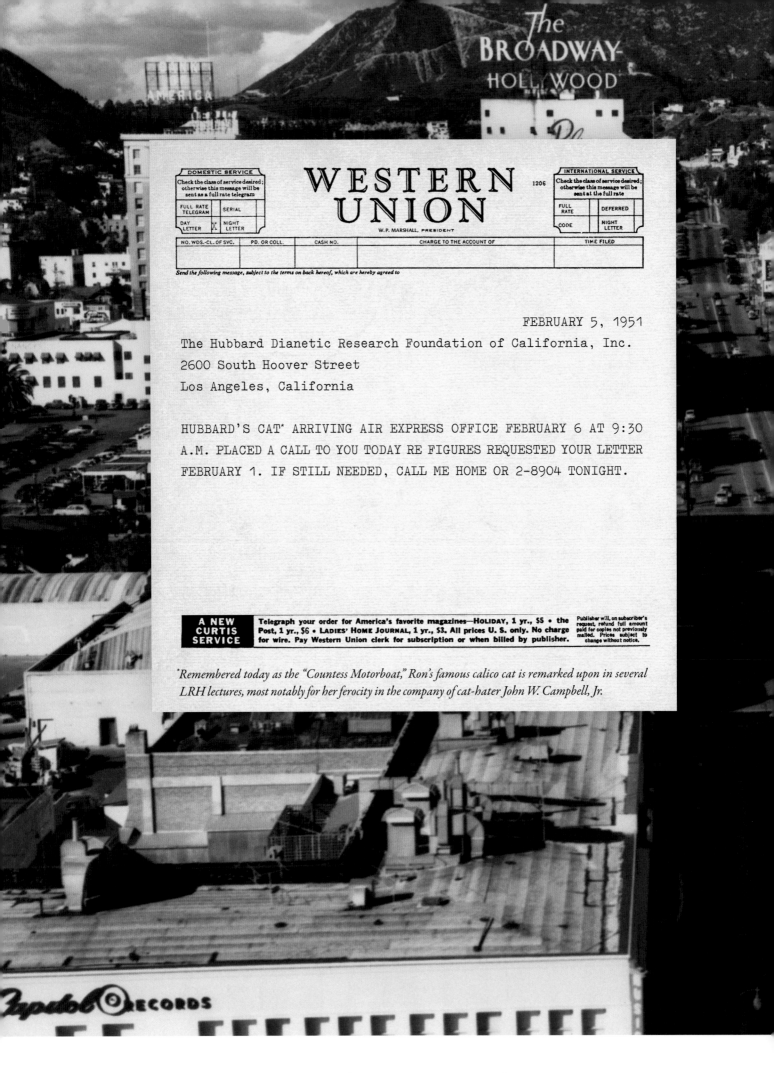

FEBRUARY 5, 1951

The Hubbard Dianetic Research Foundation of California, Inc.

2600 South Hoover Street

Los Angeles, California

HUBBARD'S CAT* ARRIVING AIR EXPRESS OFFICE FEBRUARY 6 AT 9:30
A.M. PLACED A CALL TO YOU TODAY RE FIGURES REQUESTED YOUR LETTER
FEBRUARY 1. IF STILL NEEDED, CALL ME HOME OR 2-8904 TONIGHT.

*Remembered today as the "Countess Motorboat," Ron's famous calico cat is remarked upon in several LRH lectures, most notably for her ferocity in the company of cat-hater John W. Campbell, Jr.

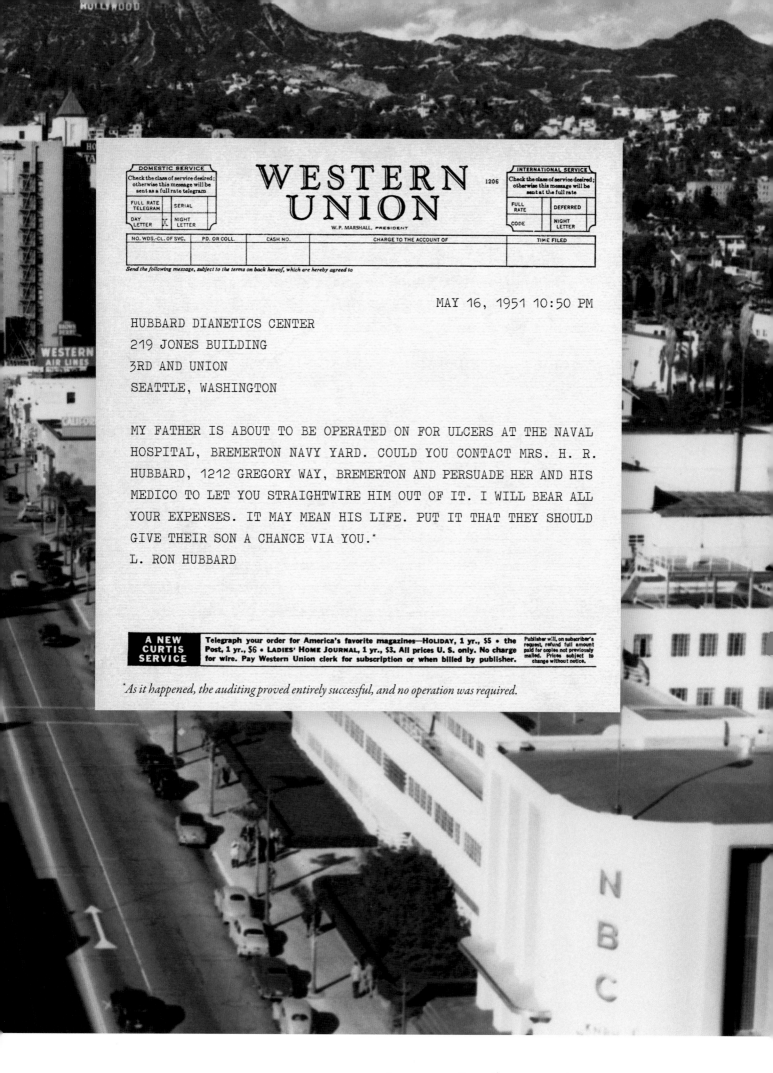

MAY 16, 1951 10:50 PM

HUBBARD DIANETICS CENTER
219 JONES BUILDING
3RD AND UNION
SEATTLE, WASHINGTON

MY FATHER IS ABOUT TO BE OPERATED ON FOR ULCERS AT THE NAVAL
HOSPITAL, BREMERTON NAVY YARD. COULD YOU CONTACT MRS. H. R.
HUBBARD, 1212 GREGORY WAY, BREMERTON AND PERSUADE HER AND HIS
MEDICO TO LET YOU STRAIGHTWIRE HIM OUT OF IT. I WILL BEAR ALL
YOUR EXPENSES. IT MAY MEAN HIS LIFE. PUT IT THAT THEY SHOULD
GIVE THEIR SON A CHANCE VIA YOU.*
L. RON HUBBARD

*As it happened, the auditing proved entirely successful, and no operation was required.

Regarding Past Lives

Among the more significant avenues of research through late 1950 was Ron's examination of past-life phenomena. The subject is, of course, extremely consequential to the continued refinement of Dianetics and all else to follow with the founding of Scientology. As regards this telling little note from December, however, the relevant facts are these: Notwithstanding the dozens of Dianeticists encountering evidence of former lives, those at the helm of the New Jersey Foundation, very much including John W. Campbell, Jr., attempted to stifle all discussion of the matter as scientifically unacceptable. (Freud and Jung dismissed it for precisely the same reason.) Nevertheless, declaring one cannot arbitrarily determine what is or is not within the human mind, LRH research continued as suggested here. The only qualification: participants in the past-life project were required to furnish their own transportation to and from the Foundation. ■

December 30, 1950

TO ANYONE INTERESTED:

In order to have to hand a test guinea pig while outlining a standard procedure on a new technique which will appear in my forthcoming book and in order to have a courier, a volunteer is requested to be with us while the book is in progress.

The volunteer's case should be of low reality level, should have had recent psychometry and little or no processing since, should be skilled in processing (in case somebody at the resort demands I process them) and should be able to run past lives and should be able to drive.

Board and room will be paid for the period the volunteer is needed, probably two to six weeks.

The volunteer is specifically informed that he is volunteering for research level study and that his case may come to harm since the study involves, in part, the restimulation but not reduction of engrams.

Anyone interested, who answers these specifications and does not mind being a martyr to science, inform Marian Adwin in the Business Office, my secretary, by 9 Tuesday morning.

L. Ron Hubbard

1/2/51
Jan Webster

Ron Hubbard

Qualifications for guinea pig:
    Low sense of reality.
    Case open and running slightly.
    Good auditor.
    Licensed driver.
    Not essential to running of Foundation as yet.
✓ Have run past deaths.
    I wish to cooperate in any way possible to further our knowledge of the science of Dianetics.
    Thanks for your attention. I hope you can use me.

Most sincerely,
Jan Webster

Left Ron's Palm Springs, California, desert home where he conducted seminal research into memories from former lives

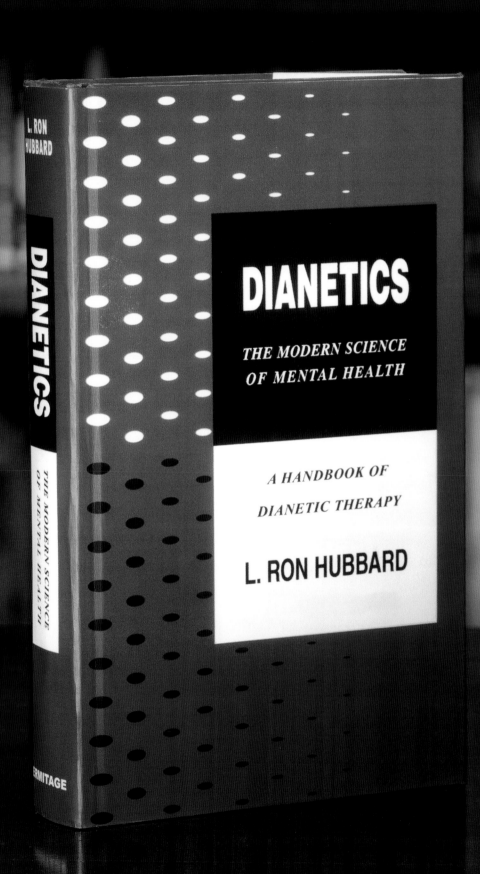

THE CASE FOR IT

by L. RON HUBBARD

THE PUBLICATION OF *Dianetics—A Handbook of Dianetic Therapy* culminates a score of years of research and intensive application. Tested on a series of 270 unselected cases, the new science produced 270 rehabilitated people, people who had been suffering, in the field of psychosomatic medicine, from arthritis, asthma, coronary difficulty, allergy, sinusitis, migraine headaches and many others and, on the mental side, from psychoses, neuroses, compulsions and repressions.

On the surface, the advent of Dianetics upon the stage of Man's knowledge may seem sudden and startlingly abrupt. A deeper inquiry demonstrates that many, many years of patient and careful work and testing were devoted to the subject prior to that release and that the science itself is made possible only by the thoughts and discoveries of thinking men. From the earliest Vedic priest, through the speculations of the early Greeks, up through the philosophies of Lucretius, Bacon, Jefferson and Spencer, through the researches of Breuer and Freud, a long trail of found facts led to a point where a single discovery could crystallize the entire field of the mind into one unified, workable whole.

With the enormous background of what may be fifty thousand years of thinking, the discovery of the actual nature of the "unconscious" mind delivered up what has proven to be an exact science for the use of Mankind and the solution of various difficulties which assail individuals.

The human mind was found to be composed of two distinct levels of ability. The "conscious" mind was discovered to be an errorless computer, inherently capable of invariably producing correct solutions insofar as its data went. However, below this "perfect" mind another mind was found. Long suspected, the sub-mind had yet never been scientifically identified nor its exact workings understood.

The "unconscious" mind was found to be the mind which was *never* "unconscious." Only the conscious mind could become "unconscious." When influenced by anesthetics as in operations or shocks or illnesses or injuries which caused "unconsciousness," the conscious mind was found to temporarily suspend operation. It was then supplanted by a mind of which it had never been aware, a cellular-level sub-mind which recorded with diabolical accuracy everything which occurred while the conscious mind was inactive. The sub-mind records sound, sight, words, touch, smell *and* pain.

An evident holdover from some past eon of Man's development, the sub-mind seeks to regulate the behavior of the body on a stimulus-response level. When the body does not obey the commands planted in it, the sub-mind then turns the pain content against the body. In that this mind cannot "think" but can only command, it easily accomplishes its moronic end of driving a person to madness at worst or aberrated errors at best. When the organism refuses to obey these commands, the sub-mind inflicts the pain which then becomes psychosomatic illness.

The commands in this sub-mind are statements made around a person when he is unconscious from anesthesia, injury, illness or shock. There is no other content in this mind.

This discovery led to a precise alignment of data about the mind and made it possible to re-evaluate early theories and select, from among the billions of items Man had collected about his mind, those facts which were useful. The result was an exact science—Dianetics.

Dianetics is easily tested and proven in any clinic or laboratory. It has been validated in universities. In that its results in the field of therapy are sweeping and permanent, it has achieved the support of all those who have investigated it thoroughly and has been opposed only by a few who have been unwilling to examine the material.

The practice of Dianetic therapy is completely nonauthoritarian and relatively simple. The most important requirements are:

1. Intelligence

2. A careful examination of the contents of the handbook

By simple we do not mean *easy*. It requires work, thought and observation. Dianetic therapy follows the natural laws of all learning processes, since Dianetics is a learning process.

EXCLUSIVE: What Drove Forrestal to Suicide?

25c
November

ANC

Why

the magazine of popular psychology

STOP PUNISHING YOURSELF
by Dr. David Fink

CAN DIANETICS HELP YOU?

THE MEN KINSEY FORGOT:
Transvestites

SEX CAN GET UNDER YOUR SKIN

WHERE TO TAKE YOUR TROUBLES

DON'T TRUST YOUR NIGHT THOUGHTS

THE TRUTH ABOUT PSYCHOANALYSIS

THE CASE OF THE BEAUTIFUL KLEPTOMANIAC

UNDERSTANDING THE FAKE HEART ATTACK:
A Case History

Self-Analysis Guide
Problem Clinic • Psycho-Photos
True Psychiatric Case Histories

Complete Book Digest

B. W. Overstreet's How to Think About Ourselves

Any two people of reasonable intelligence may work together. It cannot be done alone. Basically the technique operates as follows: the patient is asked to close his eyes and return to different experiences along his time track (the timespan of the individual from conception to present time, on which lies the sequence of events of his life) and to report his observations.

His statements of what is happening are the clues to keying-in the exact incident and the replaying of all conditions existing in the incident, which if aberrative are keeping the person or a substantial part of his personality locked up in the past. After the replaying of all the conditions recorded (on a cellular level) the pain (tension, anxiety, etc.) becomes de-intensified and the incident becomes part of the conscious experience bank of the individual, thus permitting him the use of more of himself.

This process is continued up and down the time track until all aberrative or painful incidents are de-intensified. It is not necessary to cover every phase of one's existence, since it has been discovered that many incidents are locked together. When a basic incident is contacted and de-intensified, the rest of the chain disintegrates.

Treatment of severe psychosomatic illnesses, psychoses and extreme neuroses are handled by professional therapists who may be MDs, psychiatrists and so forth, who have been specially trained to handle any emergency that may arise.

In summation, we may state that Dianetics, in addition to being a mental science for the abnormal, is primarily a mental science of the *normal*. _Ron_

"The 'conscious' mind was discovered to be an errorless computer, inherently capable of invariably producing correct solutions insofar as its data went."

CHAPTER FOUR

Letters to a
MENTAL HEALTH
MONOPOLY

...taking **U.S. by storm**

DEPENDENT NEWSPAPER FOR INDEPENDENT PEOPLE

THURS., SEPT. 7, 1950

DIANETICS

THE MODERN SCIENCE
OF MENTAL HEALTH

A HANDBOOK OF
DIANETIC THERAPY

L. RON HUBBARD

J. A. WINTER,

called emotion is really in two sections: first, there is the endocrine system which, handled either by the analytical mind ... or the reactive mind ... brings emotional responses of fear, enthusiasm, apathy, etc." Glands were an instrument of body control!

Hubbard confesses he finally tired of listening with half an ear to lectures repeating the dictums of authority while he was doing his own thinking on other planes, and he left the university sans degree.

He went on a cruise to the West Indies aboard a four-masted schooner. This was at the depth of the depression of the early 1930s and upon his return he encountered the necessity of nourishing the body as well as the mind.

...me fascinated with this as a ...y understandable phenome- ...recalls. "I wanted to learn and ...d how the mind perceives. I ...think of men as basic units ...re laid over them.

...while I discovered that what ... lying was epistemology, the ...owledge."

...this early period that Hub- ...he first came upon what is ...nderlying premise of Dianet- ...the dynamic principle of Ex-

he had begun t... he turned to th... lihood. His f... flying stories, t... and adventure fiction.

When he m... problem was d... his output. H... most prolific an... cessful writers... "I got pretty 100,000 words

He the By of th prim disc at th send book scien lang "I I did he n...

The New York Times
Book Review

NOVEMBER 12, 1950

THE BEST SELLERS

Oct. 22 Oct. 29 Nov. 5

Nonfiction Leaders
"Dianetics" — Hubbard.

World Enough and Time" — W...
Sleep Till Noon" — S...ulman
The Way West" — Guthrie.

Los Angeles Times

SUNDAY, September 17, 1950 - Part IV

BEST SELLERS

Nonfiction Leaders

1. **"Dianetics" — Hubbard.**

2. "Look Younger, Live Longer" — Hauser.

3. "Behind the Flying Saucers" — Scully.

4. "Courtroom" — Reynolds.

5. "The Little Princesses" —

...ork Times

...VIEW

...ellers

...L. Ron Hubb...

Letters to a
Mental Health
Monopoly

G IVEN ALL DIANETICS REPRESENTED AS A TRULY POPULAR challenge to a mental health monopoly and given, too, how thoroughly L. Ron Hubbard had decried the methods of that monopoly—electroconvulsive therapy, psychosurgery and massive sedation—the clash was probably inevitable. If the story has been told, the general sequence bears retelling. In the second week of May 1950, a classically clandestine effort was mounted to incorporate the subject into a United States naval program remembered today as Project Chatter. A linear descendant of Nazi experimentation at the Dachau concentration camp, the project involved the forceful altering of human behavior to expressly political ends. Precisely how Dianetics was to be employed remains unclear. But presuming one possessed the means of liberating human thought, then, perforce, one would also possess a means to the opposite, i.e., "to make men more suggestible." In either case, LRH naturally and categorically refused. In reply, a Dr. George N. Raines, then chief psychiatrist of the navy's medical institute at Bethesda, Maryland, instructed colleagues to condemn Dianetics as quackery—or as Raines specifically phrased it, he wished Dianetics to be broadly decried as "the bunk."

Much more could be said: how a crypto-psychiatric community employed federal security agencies to infiltrate the first Foundations; how interlinked publications—*Time* and *Life*, for example—were directed

Below
United States Naval Medical Institute, Bethesda, Maryland, site of secret psychiatric experimentation, circa 1949

Left Meeting with reporters from the LA *Daily News* at the Los Angeles Dianetics Foundation, September 1950

to undermine public enthusiasm for Dianetics; how an agent of the American Psychological Association attempted to force L. Ron Hubbard into a twin-engine aircraft at the Clover Field airstrip in Santa Monica and transport him to the Menninger Clinic in Topeka, Kansas, for punitive psychiatric "treatment." Then there is all one might say on the larger sociopolitical issues and all Dianetics represented to a military-industrial complex bent on what has been euphemistically described as "mass indoctrination for national security."

But rather more to the immediate point are the issues raised in Ron's reply to pop psychologist Rollo May and his "Challenge to Psychiatrists." As a word on the first, the Rollo May review of *Dianetics* was typical of psychological/psychiatric criticism of the day. Notwithstanding the fact May had never actually examined *Dianetics,* he effectively also proclaimed it "the bunk" in accordance with George Raines's party line. Meanwhile, tiring of the ping-pong match, LRH threw down the gauntlet with his crucial challenge.

Although neither the Menningers in particular, nor psychiatry in general, issued a formal response, American Psychiatric Association records are filled with memoranda on just how that challenge might be quietly and delicately sidestepped. Then, too, and as we shall see, there was yet more discussion on how Dianetics might be permanently buried for the nominal sum, six thousand dollars. ∎

Letters to the Editor
Hubbard's View

TO THE EDITOR:

Would you please ask Rollo May, who reviewed "Dianetics," to read the book? Publishing such a review gives to the public a very lopsided idea of what the professional world thinks of Dianetics. Men less emotional than Rollo May have examined the tested Dianetics.

Professors of biology, political science, sociology, psychology and physics have given Dianetics a fair and impartial survey and have discovered in it some of the answers for which they have long sought. But their opinions, as should be the case with men of science, were based on a sound investigation and applications of the science and were not warped by emotionalisms about their own economics.

The most glaring evidence that May did not study his subject before he wrote his review lies in his confusion of Dianetics with a mechanical conception of the human mind. Nowhere in the handbook of Dianetics does anyone label the human mind a machine. I fear here that May is not aware of the ridicule Dianetics has thrown upon those who always believe the

human mind was too complex to be understood. A statement that the subject of one's profession is too complex to be understood is an admission that one does not have any comprehension of his subject and it seems to me that in his review May declares himself and psychology incapable of understanding or helping in the field of humanities. Those who operate on the basic tenet that the subject of their profession cannot be understood, are operating upon a defeatist psychology.

On a subject as carefully formulated and as widely tested as Dianetics a scientific man would normally be expected to make an inquiry before expressing opinions. If he cannot bring himself to do so, then he is operating upon an emotionalism which in itself invalidates his scientific accuracy.

From medical doctors, psychiatrists and laymen the Hubbard Dianetic Research Foundation is receiving thousands upon thousands of letters which state that Dianetics has been tested and found valid, that it does precisely what it says it does. The derogatory letters are in the ratio of 1 to 505 letters of approval. Diseases and mental aberrations hitherto untouched by any past art are reported as surrendering to Dianetic techniques. Should you care to inspect the matter you will find that not one single person indulging in capricious and superficial opinionation has read fully, studied carefully or applied Dianetics.

L. Ron Hubbard
Elizabeth, N. J.

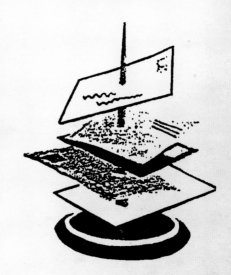

Hubbard Dianetic Research Foundation
275 Morris Ave., Elizabeth, N. J.

SPECIAL—FOR RELEASE MON., FEB. 12, 1951

DIANETICS FOUNDER
ISSUES CHALLENGE
TO PSYCHIATRISTS

Declaring that he is tired of turning the other cheek and remaining the only gentleman in what his detractors have turned into a public brawl, L. Ron Hubbard, author and founder of the new science of mental health, Dianetics, today threw down the gauntlet by issuing a challenge to the Drs. Menninger in particular and the psychiatric profession as a whole.

Long aware that organized opposition, unduly alarmed by the phenomenal spread of Dianetics, has been flailing at him "from behind the scenes and from behind the armor of their professional immunity," even inciting to legal action against the furthering of Dianetic knowledge, Hubbard has authorized the following letter to the Menninger Clinic at Topeka, Kansas, the American Psychiatric Association, and the New York Psychiatric Advancement Committee:

"The Drs. Menninger and other vocal representatives of the psychiatric field have issued such unwarranted and unfounded statements against Dianetics, having but scant knowledge of the subject, that the Hubbard Dianetic Research Foundation is compelled to submit the following for your earliest possible acceptance:

"If two impartial judges will select two neurotic persons, without advice from either psychiatrists or Dianeticists, our Foundation will be happy to give them into the hands of psychiatrists for one week, with before and after psychometries of the most rigorous nature. Thereafter our Foundation will give them Dianetic processing for one week, with comparative psychometries. If the resultant psychometries prove that Dianetics has not done uniformly more for these persons than psychiatry, Mr. Hubbard will be perfectly willing to withdraw his book, 'Dianetics,' and admit that Dianetics is not better than psychotherapy.

"This decisive test is offered in all sincerity by Mr. Hubbard and our Foundation."

Dianetics came into existence last May, following the publication of the book of that name by L. Ron Hubbard, who had been researching on the subject for 12 years. The book became an instantaneous best seller in the non-fiction field, and the vast interest

of its readers, both professional and lay, led to the creation of the Hubbard Dianetic Research Foundation, a non-profit corporation, at Elizabeth, N. J., where Hubbard resided. Subsequently, at the instigation of many who came to study under Hubbard, branch foundations were opened in New York City, Chicago, Washington, D. C., Los Angeles, Kansas City and Honolulu. Some 150 non-professional Dianetic groups and centers also formed spontaneously in the U. S., Canada, England, Scotland, Australia, Switzerland, Sweden, Denmark, Finland, France, Peru, Guatemala and the West Indies. It is estimated that, professionally or otherwise, more than a million persons are today engaged in the practice of Dianetics worldwide.

CHAPTER FIVE

A Letter from the
LAST ACT IN WICHITA

A Letter from the
Last Act in Wichita

HAVING COMPLETED A SECOND DIANETICS TEXT, *Science of Survival,* in mid-1951, Ron accepted a seemingly generous invitation to head a consolidated Dianetics Foundation in Wichita, Kansas. Extending that invitation was a somewhat ambiguous Wichita oilman by the name Don Purcell. The name initially

appears on but one of seven thousand letters received through the previous summer. Then again, this Don Purcell is vaguely recalled by students from the first New Jersey Foundation, where he briefly appeared in search of professional counseling. But his late April offer to provide L. Ron Hubbard with a financially independent Foundation and all else necessary for the advancement of Dianetics was, on the whole, unprecedented.

The arrangement essentially called for LRH research and lectures at an equitable salary, while Purcell attended to financial concerns—even including the assumption of debts from an overextended Elizabeth Foundation. In what amounted to a small formality, Purcell was to further assume a nominal hold on the copyrights of Dianetics, but only for a limited period.

Initially all proceeded as described. Dianeticists uprooted themselves from New Jersey, Chicago, New York and Los Angeles, and LRH commenced instruction in a neatly appointed West Douglas Avenue hall. Meanwhile research continued into that most fascinating realm of past-life phenomena, chronicled today in *Scientology: A History of Man.* Then quite without warning, the curtain fell with a midafternoon announcement of bankruptcy.

Details are complex, but for the sake of simplicity the sequence was essentially this: On what amounted to a fabricated claim, Purcell had plunged his Wichita Foundation into bankruptcy. LRH, in turn, found himself served with several writs and demands for equity, although, as he so succinctly put it: "They obviously do not want my car or my cash.

An early lecture on advanced auditing techniques at the Dianetics Foundation in Wichita, Kansas, 1951

Below
E. E. Manney's Wichita Publishing Company, where numerous early Dianetics and Scientology books were originally printed

Right
Science of Survival: prediction of human behavior

And they obviously want my copyrights, the name HUBBARD, the word DIANETICS and Dianetics processes.... And this is obviously no bankruptcy but a scheme to place me in such straits and hurt me so much that I will be forced to give them all they seek."

And it was true—every word of it. For having succeeded in his plunging the corporation into bankruptcy, Purcell casually cut a $6,124 check and purchased fifteen oak side chairs, thirteen arm side chairs, nineteen inkwells and pens, ten thousand copies of *Science of Survival*—and for the same six thousand dollars—the names and copyrights for both Dianetics and L. Ron Hubbard. While just for good measure (and altogether more to the point), Purcell further received a most mysterious fifty thousand dollars from an undisclosed medical/psychiatric slush fund.

So it was, in a perfectly brilliant and droll reply, Ron authored his wry letter on the "last acts from the comic opera." It dates from the spring of 1952 and was addressed to a court in Phoenix, Arizona, where he had founded a new Hubbard College (not to mention Scientology). It ultimately played precisely as intended and all copyrights and trademarks were indeed soon returned to L. Ron Hubbard. ▪

Science of Survival

SIMPLIFIED, FASTER
DIANETIC TECHNIQUES

by **L. Ron Hubbard**

ONE OF THE LAST ACTS
FROM THE COMIC OPERA

On May 10 I got a letter saying I better pay off some money to a fellow named Purcell in Wichita and I better pay it by the 13th. Well, I knowed I didn't owe this here money but my house had been ransacked in Wichita and the paper saying I didn't owe it got stolen and I knowed there was a note with my name on it I signed way back last fall.

And I told my attorney and he said he'd do something about it but this firm that writ me the letter, name of Evans and Hull and things, said epistle being signed by a Boland, they'd already sued in Superior court and that's bad for my repute and my business.

And on May 16 this here Boland served a process on my attorney but I guess Boland needed processing, not me, because Boland, soon as he got through talking to my attorney, he called me up and he said now he had me and all this was criminal owing a note and things and I better get down to his office right away or something bad would happen so I went. And he said not to bring any attorney or nothing so I didn't.

And I got in there and this here Boland was in an office in the office of EVANS KITCHEL HULL and things, an attorney firm that ain't so firm now, and this Boland he flashed a note on me and at long range it seemed it was my note. And this Boland didn't have nobody with him but I had a couple friends with me so I'm glad because I got the witnesses in my favor because this Boland was pretty rough and he said he had some more suits and if I didn't pay the note right then he'd sue and enjoin and ruin me and if I did pay he'd give me this here note he was waving around, and if I didn't pay him there was plenty of criminal charges around and he'd get at least one of my associates put in the cooler.

And I guess I got pretty rattled so I just up and give him a check and said it would be good on next Tuesday and he said ok and I give him all I thought I would have in the bank by Tuesday the 20th and then about sixty cash and this here Boland he said "Now when I get the cash you can have this note" and he already had my check. But I had witnesses and I said he better give me the note.

Well sir, this here Boland he looked pretty sick but I kept saying that he hadda give me the note and so he finally up and writ on it what I'd paid and he signed it. And he give it to me but he said he'd dismiss the suit and things agin me but not to go paradin' around tellin' people about it or showin' the note around and I better burn it and then it couldn't git away.

So I turn loose the corner of my four thousand dollar check which been holdin' the corner of and I went out in the street where the light was better and I look at this here note and by DING it warn't my signature.

And I take this note and I look at it careful and by DING it ain't the right date but later'n the right date and so I go look up one of these handwritin' fellers that tells signatures and give it to him and I go to the phone and I try to call this here Boland but this here Boland he ain't to be reached nowhere. And so I go down and I put a stop and halt in the name of the law order on that there check I give because whar I come from passin' off docyments that's been enforgerated is forgery or grand forgery of the first degree or fraudulent practice and it's frowned on.

And it was all mighty surprising to me, this here Boland bein' part like he was of the firm of EVANS HULL KITCHEL AND JENCKES and they havin' accounts and bein' the lawyers of THE SOUTHERN PACIFIC RAILROAD and a lot of companies I'm lookin' up so I can mention them to show how surprised I was about the forgery.

And the next mornin' I go to the bank first thing just as soon as the doors git open and I got money on me, namely $880 dullars to deposit just to make purty sure there was all the money there needed to be in the bank when that there check was presented because I hear it's illegal to not have the money to make up the check sum.

But here was this Boland and I guess he come in the letter slot or through the cracks because He's already chawin' the eear of the bank manager about the check even though he'd promised me to wait 'til Tuesday. And this Boland he looks worried.

And this here Boland sees me and he beelines over and he says pretty threatenin' like that if I don't take off that there stop order he'll have me all ways for Sunday. And I say is he sure it was a good note and he says that don't make any account, I better give him the money or he'll put me in a lot of trouble like suin' me for libel and even puttin' one of my associates name of ELLIOTT in jail afore sundown for any kind of a charge such as GRAND LARCENY or anything. And I say ELLIOTT would have to be guilty of somethin' afore you could arrest him and he ain't guilty of nothin' except the unwiseness of bein' my associate when guys like Boland is loose. And this Boland he says he can do anything. He says Purcell says he owns the police of Wichita and Boland he controls the police of Phoenix and they can do anything and no court's big enough to stop 'em. And I say I can't believe it.

Well, sir, sure enough, this here ELLIOTT he's in jail the very next evening just like Boland said. A call come through from Wichita to the Phoenix police and there's been a warrant out for Elliott nobody knows anything about and here BANG it's served just like Boland predictepated. And Elliott he got to post bond and they tie up his car and I can't figure it because they got Elliott charged for stealin' property which I got in good American writin' is entirely mine, but they say it ain't mine now because Elliott stole it but Elliott, he couldn't steal from me because he can have anything I got anyway.

But come Monday, May 19, this here Boland has jumped into court with this stop-payment check even though he's wised up that I don't like his passin' off a forgery on me for good American money AND a check, and Elliott, he got fingerprinted but later we got somebody in Wichita to investigate and by golly the Phoenix police had to give back Elliott's bond and his car and his fingerprints and everything, so Elliott got out of it. But this here Boland, he jumps around and phones me that this ain't all. He says he'll sue me for everything he can think up because this here firm EVANS, HULL KITCHEL AND JENCKES that is retained by so many big companies like THE SOUTHERN PACIFIC RAILROAD and the rest I'm getting a list complete so I'll know and can be impressed better, this Boland says they own the cops and the sheriff and I better come through with cash or they'll arrest me next on anything they can think up.

And they start orderin' my attorney around and they are pretty wild. And all this is very confusin' to me because seems like to me this Boland and EVANS etc. that is hired by so many big firms like THE SOUTHERN PACIFIC RAILROAD, can't be the law in Arizona even so. And it seems like when people pass off forged notes and threaten and take money for false documents and put people in fear and use threat and duress to collect civil bills and arrest people so they can be let off for a price and sue a lot of suits

that ain't so just to spoil somebody's business and collect a note that wasn't really owed, why it seems like there's SOME provision in this here law book that says it ain't quite legal—that it's at least a misdemeanor or something you take to the CIVIL LIBERTIES UNION or congress or somewhere. And even if like they say they own all the law in Arizona, seems like somebody ought to put a mortgage on some of it.

And thinkin' it over real close, bein' pretty dumb legal wise, looks like this Boland and this Evans etc. that owns the SOUTHERN PACIFIC RAILROAD or at least retains it, why it seems like they ought to at least get a traffic ticket for blockin' the road.

What do *you* think, judge?

Epilogue
A Book Called Dianetics

In celebration of the thirty-first anniversary of *Dianetics: The Modern Science of Mental Health,* L. Ron Hubbard penned the following on 15 April 1981:

31 years ago this May
A message was given to this place.

A book called Dianetics
Struck the blow
That blew the bars
Of ignorance away.

But men
Who would oppress
Have labored hard to reconstruct
Their barricade.

For if all men
Were to go free
What then would jackals use for prey?

You have a trust to forward on
The work that
Was begun
And with the tramp of many feet
Stamp wide the path we won.

Each year that flows behind us finds
Less force in the dismay
That met us thirty-one years ago
Upon the ninth of May.

Oh yes, we'll win for Mankind yet
His right to truth, true wealth.
Why let him die
When he can have
Dianetics and mental health?

It's up to you
To see that Man
Continues on his way.

Do all you can
My friends to see
That freedom wins the day.

APPENDIX

GLOSSARY

A

aberrant: deviating from the ordinary, usual or normal; abnormal. Page 1.

aberrate(d): affected by *aberration,* a departure from rational thought or behavior. From the Latin, *aberrare,* to wander from; Latin, *ab,* away, and *errare,* to wander. It means basically to err, to make mistakes, or more specifically to have fixed ideas which are not true. The word is also used in its scientific sense. It means departure from a straight line. If a line should go from A to B, then if it is "aberrated" it would go from A to some other point, to some other point, to some other point, to some other point, to some other point and finally arrive at B. Taken in its scientific sense, it would also mean the lack of straightness or to see crookedly, as an example, a man sees a horse but thinks he sees an elephant. Aberrated conduct would be wrong conduct, or conduct not supported by reason. Page 1.

abiding: continuing without change; enduring; lasting. Page 15.

accident-prone: a person likely to cause or attract an accident, more than the average person. Page 31.

account, that don't make any: an informal expression meaning "that is not important." Page 117.

accruing: coming about as an increase or accumulation. Page 82.

adage: a traditional saying expressing a common experience or observation; a proverb. Page 44.

Adler: Alfred Adler (1870–1937), Austrian psychologist and psychiatrist; he broke with Freud (1911) by stressing that a sense of inferiority, rather than sexual drive, is the motivating force in human life. Page 25.

advent: arrival of something important. Page 1.

aeronautics: the science, art, theory and practice of designing, building and operating aircraft. Page 15.

afore: an earlier word used to mean *before*. Page 117.

agin: an informal term for *against*. Page 41.

air express: a fast, direct service for shipping small packages of goods by air. It includes ground pickup at origin and delivery at destination. Page 94.

albeit: although; even if. Page vii.

Algiers: a seaport in and the capital and largest city of Algeria in northwestern Africa, on the Mediterranean Sea. Page 38.

alleviate: lighten or lessen; become easier to endure. Page 32.

allied: having to do with the *Allies,* in World War II (1939–1945), the twenty-six nations that fought against the Axis (Germany, Italy and Japan, often with Bulgaria, Hungary and Romania). The term *Allies* especially applies to Great Britain, the United States and the former Soviet Union. Page 38.

altruistic: unselfishly concerned for or devoted to the welfare of others. Page 35.

ambiguous: unreliable or vague and unclear as to intentions, activities, etc. Page 113.

American Medical Association: a professional physicians' organization in the United States, founded in 1847 and composed of state and county medical associations. Page 16.

American Psychiatric Association: national society of psychiatrists founded in 1844 as the Association of Medical Superintendents of American Institutions for the Insane. Page 16.

American Psychological Association: an American association of psychologists founded in 1892. Page 106.

amnesia trance: a deep sleeplike state of consciousness that makes a person susceptible to commands. *Amnesia* in this sense refers to the fact that the person normally does not remember what took place during the deep trance state. Page 30.

amply: to an extent that is considerably more than adequate or enough; abundantly. Page 45.

analogous: comparable in certain respects; alike or similar. Page 28.

analytical mind: that mind which computes—the "I" and his consciousness. Page 28.

ancillary: supplying something additional, such as data or information. Page 7.

anemia: a condition of the blood in which there are too few red blood cells, resulting in breathlessness, weakness, etc. Page 74.

anesthesia: a partial or total loss of the senses of feeling, as pain, heat, cold, touch, etc. Page 28.

anesthetized: made unconscious as by an *anesthetic,* a substance that brings about unconsciousness or insensitivity to pain. Page 72.

antiquate: make obsolete or out-of-date by replacing with something newer or better. Page 76.

AP: an abbreviation for *Associated Press,* a large United States news agency that gathers and distributes foreign and domestic news and photographs to member newspapers, television and radio stations around the world. Page 51.

append: attach or fasten (something to something else). Page 29.

appointed: decorated; furnished or equipped with things that are needed. Page 113.

apprehension(s): a feeling of fear that something bad may happen; anxiety. Page 45.

apropos of: with regard to; concerning. Page 42.

Arabian Nights: or *A Thousand and One Nights,* a collection of stories from Persia, Arabia, India and Egypt, compiled over hundreds of years. They include the stories of Aladdin and Ali Baba and have become particularly popular in Western countries. Page 35.

arbiter: a person who has the power and authority to settle a dispute or decide an issue. Page 81.

Archives: collections of documents, such as letters, official papers, photographs, diaries or recorded materials. Page vii.

arena: a field of interest, activity or the like. Page 70.

aristocracy: any class or group considered to be superior, as through education, ability, wealth or social prestige. Page 44.

arrested: slowed down or stopped. Page 20.

arthritis: inflammation of the joints, causing pain, swelling and stiffness. Page 20.

article: a word that tells whether a speaker or writer is referring to a specific person, place or thing (for example, *the* dog) or whether he's referring to any one person, place or thing out of a general group (for example, *a* dog). Page 80.

ASF: an abbreviation for *Astounding Science Fiction* magazine. Page 24.

assail: impinge upon; trouble; invade or attack; overwhelm the mind. Page 99.

Associate Membership: a membership with the Hubbard Dianetic Research Foundation of the early 1950s, open to individuals interested in Dianetics. Associate Members received information on all new developments in Dianetics through a bulletin issued periodically to members only. Page 71.

Astounding Science Fiction: a magazine founded in 1930 that featured adventure stories and, later, science fiction. The May 1950 issue featured one of the first articles on Dianetics, *Dianetics: The Evolution of a Science.* Page 16.

Ast. Science Fiction: an abbreviation for *Astounding Science Fiction* magazine. Page 51.

Atabrine: a brand name for a synthetic drug used in the treatment of malaria. Page 29.

athlete's foot: a fungal infection of the feet in which the skin becomes itchy and cracked or peels off. Page 8.

auditing: applying Dianetics techniques (called *processes*). Processes are directly concerned with increasing the ability of the individual to survive, with increasing his sanity or ability to reason, his physical ability and his general enjoyment of life. Page 1.

auditor: the individual who administers Dianetic therapy. To audit means "to listen" and also "to compute." Page 43.

Auditor's Code: a collection of rules (do's and don'ts) that an auditor follows while auditing someone, which ensures that the preclear will get the greatest possible gain out of the processing that he is having. Page 67.

aura: a sensation, such as of voices, colored lights or numbness, experienced before an attack of epilepsy, migraine or certain other nervous system disorders. Page 66.

axiomatic: self-evident; obviously true. Page 72.

axioms: statements of natural laws on the order of those of the physical sciences, especially the Dianetic Axioms. Page 27.

B

backlash: a strong, adverse reaction to something. Page 3.

Bacon: Francis Bacon (1561–1626), influential English philosopher who believed that any bias or prejudice in scientific thinking must be abandoned and that accurate observation and experimentation were vital to science. He helped develop the scientific method of solving problems. Page 99.

Baltimore: a city of northern Maryland, an eastern state of the United States. Page 16.

bank on: base one's hopes or confidence on. Page 17.

Banks Islander: a native or inhabitant of the *Banks Island,* an island of northwestern Canada in the Arctic Ocean. Relying on shamans for spiritual interpretation, some inhabitants believed they could see spirits of their ancestors or friends in the next life by looking into the *northern lights,* the colored lights seen in the skies of northern regions. *See also* **shamanism.** Page 31.

bar association: an organization of lawyers established to promote professional competence, enforce standards of ethical conduct and encourage a spirit of public service among members of the legal profession. Page 76.

barbarism: an action of extreme cruelty or brutality. Page 32.

basic-basic: the first engram after conception, the basic of all chains by sole virtue of being the first moment of pain. Page 85.

Bay Head: a town on the Atlantic coast of the United States, in the state of New Jersey, about 70 miles (110 kilometers) south of New York City. Page 3.

bears: calls for; requires. Page 105.

beat: in journalism, a reporting of a news item ahead of all rivals. Page 42.

Beaumont, Texas: a city and port in southeastern Texas connected to the Gulf of Mexico by a ship canal. Page 70.

Beaux-Arts: the *École Nationale Supérieure des Beaux-Arts,* the National Superior School of Fine Arts in Paris, France, founded in the 1600s. The Beaux-Arts offers classes in drawing, painting, engraving and sculpture, open to those who qualify after taking examinations. The professors at the school are selected from the most able of French artists and the high standards maintained by the Beaux-Arts have influenced both American and European artists. Page 7.

bedridden: forced to remain in bed because of illness, weakness or injury. Page 1.

beelines: goes straight toward (someone or something) as quickly and directly as possible. Page 117.

Beethoven Ninth: the ninth and last symphony written by German composer Ludwig van Beethoven (1770–1827), completed in 1824. The first movement is the first of the symphony's four sections. (A *symphony* is an elaborate composition written for an orchestra and usually of grand proportion and varied elements. Most symphonies are instrumental only; the Beethoven Ninth includes a final section with chorus.) Page 66.

beheld: observed; perceived. Page 80.

belabor: subject somebody to a sustained verbal or literary outburst. Page 38.

bells, 4: *bell* is a nautical term meaning any of the half-hour units of time rung on the bell of a ship during a *watch,* a four-hour period of time during which assigned personnel of the ship are on duty. The first watch is midnight to 4 A.M. and during this watch, one bell indicates 12:30 A.M., two bells indicate 1:00 A.M., three bells indicate 1:30 A.M. and four bells indicate 2 A.M. Page 52.

bent: strongly inclined; determined to take a course of action, usually with the word *on* or *upon.* Page 106.

Benzedrine: brand name of a drug that increases physical and mental activity, prevents sleep and decreases appetite. Page 30.

Bering: the Bering Sea, located in the northernmost part of the Pacific Ocean, separating the continents of Asia and North America. Named after Danish navigator Vitus Bering (1680–1741). Page 54.

Bethesda, Maryland: a suburb of the state of Maryland, located northwest of Washington, DC. Page 105.

bit off a trifle more than it had bargained for: a variation of the phrase *bite off more than one can chew,* try to do more than had been initially anticipated or taken into account. Page 32.

blazing: figuratively, of tremendous intensity, great warmth and earnestness of feeling, likened to a fire burning brightly and with great force. Page 45.

blissful: full of happiness; perfectly happy. Page 56.

blood-stained: involved with slaughter, murder or bloodshed; stained with blood. Page 80.

boil-off: the manifestation of former periods of unconsciousness, accompanied by grogginess. In its English usage, *boil-off* refers to the reduction in quantity of a liquid by its conversion to a gaseous state, such as steam. Page 86.

bombast: figuratively, a term used to mean a strongly worded criticism, likened to a bomb exploding. Page 43.

bond, post: submit money to be left with a court of law as security to make sure that a defendant, while not imprisoned, complies with the directions and orders of a court or other authorized official and appears before the court when required. Page 118.

bone of contention: a subject that causes disagreement or argument. Page 42.

Book One: *Dianetics: The Modern Science of Mental Health,* the basic text on Dianetics techniques, written by L. Ron Hubbard and first published in 1950. It is also referred to as the First Book. Page 3.

bottom of my heart, from the: very sincerely or deeply. Page 10.

bout: an attack of something, such as an illness or a period of time taken up by such. Page 62.

Brass Tacks: a regularly occurring section of *Astounding Science Fiction* magazine devoted to readers' letters. *Brass tacks* is an informal term meaning the basic facts or practical details. Page 37.

brawl: a rough and noisy fight, usually in a public place and one involving a large number of people. Page 108.

break: (of news) suddenly become public. Page 54.

breath of Hell, feel the hot: a reference to a near-death experience, as if one was so close to the fires of Hell that he could feel the scorching hot air emanating from within. Page 38.

Bremerton: a city in western Washington, a state in the northwest United States, on the Pacific coast. The large US Naval Yard in Bremerton was established in 1891 and provides maintenance for every class of naval vessel. Page 95.

Breuer: Josef Breuer (1842–1925), Austrian physician who worked closely with Sigmund Freud in the 1880s and attempted to relieve neurosis in patients by use of hypnosis. Page 99.

brickbat(s): literally, a piece of broken brick thrown as a weapon. Figuratively, a *brickbat* is an uncomplimentary remark, especially an insult or criticism. Page 43.

broach: mention or suggest for the first time. Page 66.

broke (something) out: pulled out of storage with the intention of putting to use. Page 17.

brow: the top edge of a hill or the highest part of a slope. Page 38.

brunt, carry the: take on or bear the main burden or responsibility. Page 89.

B-17: a large bomber aircraft, also known as the *Flying Fortress,* built by the Boeing Aircraft Company and first used in combat in the early 1940s. The B-17 (*B* standing for *bomber*) was used extensively by the United States during World War II (1939–1945). Each B-17 carried approximately four tons of bombs. Page 38.

bulletins: publications issued by the Hubbard Dianetic Research Foundation in mid-1950, containing technical and research data. Page 82.

bunk, the: complete nonsense or something that is not true. Page 105.

C

calico cat: a cat with a coat marked with spots of black, brown, yellow or orange. Originally, *calico* referred to a type of cotton cloth from India, with a bright printed pattern. Page 94.

California Veterans Administration: the agency charged with administering benefits provided by law for veterans of the armed forces in California. Page 15.

cameo role: literally, a small part that stands out from other minor parts, as in a play or film, performed by a distinguished actor. Used figuratively to refer to a brief appearance by a prominent person. *Cameo* refers to a type of jewelry made by carving a precious stone so that the raised design, often a head in profile, stands out as a different color than the background. Page 49.

Campbell, Jr., John W.: (1910–1971) American editor and writer who began writing science fiction while at college. In 1937 Campbell was appointed editor of the magazine *Astounding Stories,* later titled *Astounding Science Fiction* and then *Analog.* Under his editorship *Astounding* became a major influence in the development of science fiction and published stories by some of the most important writers of that time. Page 8.

cap: provide a fitting climax or conclusion to. Page 34.

capital: wealth that a person or organization owns and that can be invested, lent or borrowed. Page 54.

capricious: tending to change unpredictably or abruptly with no apparent reason; erratic. Page 28.

carry on their own energy: sustain the weight or burden of, by means of one's vital impulse or life force. Page 44.

Casbah: the older section of the city of Algiers, capital city of the North African country of Algeria, consisting of winding, mazelike patterns of streets and close, crowded buildings. This section was named for the fortress (casbah) that exists in the area. During World War II (1939–1945), Algiers was the headquarters of the Allied forces in North Africa. Page 38.

categorically: absolutely, certainly and unconditionally, with no room for doubt, question or contradiction. Page 105.

cellular: having to do with a *cell,* the smallest structural unit of an organism that is capable of independent functioning. All plants and animals are made up of one or more cells that usually combine to form various tissues. Page 100.

censures: criticizes; expresses strong disapproval of. Page 72.

Ceppos, Arthur (Art): (1910–1997) founder and former president of Hermitage House, the first publisher of *Dianetics: The Modern Science of Mental Health.* Page 34.

Channel: a reference to the *English Channel,* the body of water between England and France that connects the Atlantic Ocean with the North Sea, 350 miles (563 kilometers) long and between 21 and 100 miles (34 and 160 kilometers) wide. Page 38.

charity case(s): a person who is not able to pay for service or is otherwise in need of assistance and who is provided help by an organization voluntarily or free of charge. Page 89.

chart: literally, a map for the use of navigators, showing a portion of the sea and indicating the outline of the coasts, the position of rocks, sandbanks, channels, etc. Also used figuratively to mean a plan or outline that lays out a course of action. Page 32.

chase down: pursue (something, such as a goal or target) in order to observe, obtain or discover. Page 32.

chatty: characterized by friendly and informal talk or writing, often about minor or personal matters. Page 84.

chawin' the eear: a spelling that represents an informal pronunciation of *chewing the ear,* talking to someone energetically or at length. Page 117.

cheek, turning the other: accepting injuries or insult without seeking revenge; refusing to retaliate. Page 108.

Choccolocco, Alabama: a small town located in northeastern Alabama, a state in the southeastern United States. Page 67.

chord, struck a responsive: a variation of *struck the right note,* meaning said or did something that produced a desired answer or effect. Page 59.

chronicled: recorded or recounted, as in a historical record of facts or events, in the order they happened. Page 113.

cited: mentioned, especially as an example of what one is saying. Page 50.

civil: of citizens; relating to what happens within a state or between different citizens or groups of citizens within the state. Page 118.

Civil Liberties Union: in full, the American Civil Liberties Union (ACLU), an organization founded in 1920 and headquartered in New York City. It is devoted to defending the rights and freedoms of people in the United States as covered in the US Constitution. It works mainly by providing lawyers and legal advice for individuals and groups in local, state and federal courts. Page 119.

clandestine: secret or hidden, with an intent to conceal. Page 105.

clash: a conflict, as between differing interests, views or purposes. Page 105.

clause: a distinct section of a document, especially an official or formal document, covering a particular subject, condition, etc., that is usually separately numbered. Page 61.

Clear: a being who no longer has his own reactive mind. He is a person who is not affected by aberration (any deviation or departure from rationality). He is rational in that he forms the best possible solutions he can on the data he has and from his viewpoint. Page 44.

Clearing: the action of deleting (clearing) from the reactive mind all physically painful experiences that have resulted in the aberration of the analytical mind. Page 30.

Clearwater: a city in western Florida (a southeastern state in the United States), near St. Petersburg and Tampa. Page 74.

clinical: purely scientific. Also, based on actual observation of individuals rather than theory. Page 19.

Clover Field airstrip: the original name of Santa Monica Airport, a public airport in the city of Santa Monica in Southern California, near Los Angeles. The airport was one of the first in the region and the site of aircraft manufacture during World War II (1939–1945). Page 106.

coda: in some pieces of music, a more or less independent passage added to the end of a section to reinforce the sense of conclusion, often adding dramatic energy to the work. Page 66.

colitis: inflammation of the colon, characterized by lower-bowel spasms and upper-abdominal cramps. Page 51.

colloquial: characteristic of or appropriate to ordinary or familiar conversation rather than formal speech or writing; informal. Page 82.

column: a series of feature articles regularly appearing in a newspaper or magazine by a particular writer or about a certain subject. Page 8.

comatose: in a state of deep unconsciousness for a prolonged or indefinite period, especially as a result of severe injury or illness. Page 72.

comic opera: a term used to distinguish operas that are lighter in style than a serious opera. Not necessarily humorous, comic operas generally deal with ordinary people and places and end happily as compared to serious operas, which deal with mythological or historical subjects and typically end tragically. In a comic opera singing generally alternates with passages that are half-sung and half-spoken. Page 116.

commenced: began happening or began something. Page 7.

commercialism: emphasis on the financial profit of something. Page 89.

Committee on Evidence: a committee responsible for determining what type of evidence should or should not be considered allowable or valid in judicial proceedings. Page 76.

complex(es): in psychoanalysis, a group of interrelated impulses, ideas and emotions of which the individual is unaware, but which strongly influence his attitudes, feelings and behavior in a particular activity. Page 17.

complication(s): a secondary disease or condition aggravating an already existing one. Page 66.

complimentary: giving or containing a compliment; expressing courtesy, respect, admiration or praise. Page 29.

compulsion: the state or condition of being compelled (overpowered); an irresistible impulse that is irrational or contrary to one's own will. Page 99.

conducive to: tending to produce; contributive. Page 56.

congrats: a shortening of *congratulations,* used as an informal way of expressing one's pleasure to someone for an achievement or good fortune or on a special occasion. Page 52.

conjecture(s): the formation or expression of an opinion or theory without sufficient evidence or proof. Page 57.

connotes: implies or suggests; indicates. Page 81.

consequential: of importance; bringing about or responsible for significant changes or results. Page 96.

consolidated: joined or brought together into a single unit, said of activities, organizations, businesses, etc. Page 113.

contagious: spreading or tending to spread from one person to another, likened to a disease that is transmitted by direct or indirect bodily contact. Page 30.

convulsion(s): a period of violent social or political stress, strain and confusion. Page 81.

cool: become free from excitement, strong feelings or the like. Page 56.

cooler, the: a slang term for *prison.* Page 116.

Coord. Council: short for *Coordination Council,* the name of a Dianetics group active in Los Angeles, California, in 1950. Page 86.

copyright: the exclusive right given by law for a certain term of years to an author, composer, designer, etc., to print, publish and sell copies of his original work. Page 113.

coronary: a disease of the coronary (heart) arteries and veins or conditions associated with it. Page 32.

cosmic consciousness: the belief that the cosmos (the life and order of the universe) brings about intellectual enlightenment that puts the individual on a new plane of existence, accompanied with a feeling of elevation, elation and a concept of immortality. Put forth by Canadian psychiatrist R. M. Bucke. Page 69.

couched: expressed in a particular style or with a particular choice of words. Page 41.

covetous: having a strong desire to possess something, especially something that belongs to another person. Page 3.

crevasse: a deep crack, for example, in the ice of a glacier. Page 28.

crypto-: hidden or secret, used in forming compound words: *crypto-psychiatric.* Page 105.

crystallize: give definite or concrete form to; make fixed or definite. Page 99.

cursory: going rapidly over something, without discussing details. Page 30.

curtain fell, the: the show came to an end, as in a theatrical performance where the stage curtain is lowered to indicate the performance is over. Used figuratively. Page 113.

curtain raiser: a preliminary event. Originally, a short opening piece performed before the principal play of the evening. (From the idea of a stage curtain being raised at the start of a performance.) Page 34.

cybernetics: the comparison between the communication and control systems of living organisms and automated machines such as computers. For example, by studying how the mind and nervous systems work, one could then reproduce that "thinking process" in a computer. Page 31.

D

Dachau (concentration camp): a German concentration camp organized in 1933 and ended in 1945. It held more than 160,000 slave laborers and had facilities for mass murder and cremation of the camp's inmates. It was also a medical research center where experiments were carried out on more than 3,500 inmates. Dachau is a town 10 miles (16 kilometers) northwest of Munich, Germany. Page 105.

Dallas Morning News: a major daily newspaper serving Dallas, Texas. Texas is a state in the southwestern US. Page 79.

decided: certain and unquestionable. Page 20.

decisive: that settles or can settle a dispute, question, etc.; conclusive. Page 108.

decried: publicly declared to be wrong or evil; denounced. Page 105.

deep space: a term for the regions of space that are beyond the *solar system,* the Sun and the group of planets that move around it. Page 34.

defeatist: characterized by an attitude of giving up easily or of not being able to succeed at something. Page 107.

defunct: not operating or functioning; no longer in existence. Page 98.

degree, of the first: of the highest level; the most extreme or serious of its kind. Page 117.

de-intensified: reduced in strength or intensity; freed from strong sensation, emotion, feelings, etc. Page 101.

delirium: a state marked by extreme restlessness, confusion and sometimes hallucinations, caused by fever, poisoning or brain injury. Page 28.

delusion: a persistent false belief or opinion that is resistant to reason and confrontation with actual fact. Page 81.

delusions of grandeur: a false belief concerning one's personality or status, which is thought to be more important than it is. Page 58.

demon circuits: in Dianetics, a "demon" is a parasitic circuit. It has an action in the mind which approximates another entity than self and was considered in Dianetics to be derived entirely from words in engrams. Their phenomena are described in *Dianetics: The Modern Science of Mental Health*. Page 85.

denouncement: an act of criticizing or condemning something publicly and harshly. Page 42.

dense: difficult to understand or follow. Page 58.

deprivation: the state of being without something, especially of being without adequate food or shelter. Page 31.

despoil: steal valuable or attractive possessions from (a place). Page 81.

detractors: persons that speak ill of or try to lessen the value or importance of. Page 108.

diabolical: extreme or exceedingly great in degree. Page 100.

Dianetics Foundation(s): a reference to the Hubbard Dianetic Research Foundation, the first organization of Dianetics, formed in 1950 in Elizabeth, New Jersey, or the branch foundations in other US cities. Their purpose was to further Dianetics research and, mainly, to offer training. Page 61.

Dianetics—A Handbook of Dianetic Therapy: a reference to *Dianetics: The Modern Science of Mental Health,* published in 1950. The original cover of the book contained the subtitle *A Handbook of Dianetic Therapy*. Page 99.

Dieppe: a city and port in northern France. During World War II (1939–1945), the Germans occupied Dieppe, transforming it into one of the most strongly fortified points on the English Channel. In August 1942, to obtain data for a subsequent invasion of Europe, the Allies staged a raid during which heavy casualties were sustained. Page 38.

Dilantin: a drug used to treat the seizures or violent muscle contractions caused by epilepsy. Page 66.

dilated: with the pupil widened or expanded so that more light is admitted into the eye. Page 73.

diluting: making something weaker, less efficient or less forceful by modifying it or adding other elements. Page 45.

ding: a milder expression replacing the word *damn*. Page 117.

dingy: lacking light in a gloomy or unpleasant way. Page 8.

disbanding: the action of breaking up a group by dismissing its members; for example, when the group has completed a planned assignment. Page 27.

disclosing: revealing or making known. Page 29.

disheartened: made less hopeful or enthusiastic. Page 44.

disintegrates: breaks up or falls apart, so as to be destroyed. Page 101.

dismiss: formally put a legal action out of court; refuse to give further hearing to a case (in court). Page 116.

dissertation: a written communication about a subject, in which it is discussed at length. Page 72.

disservice: an action that causes harm or difficulty; the opposite of *service,* which is work done for somebody else to help them. Page 52.

doc(s): an informal term for a *doctor.* Page 10.

docyment(s): a spelling that represents an informal or humorous pronunciation of *document.* Page 117.

dope: an informal term for information, data or news. Page 85.

dormant: temporarily without activity, energy, power or effect. Page 28.

dose, stiff: an amount of something regarded as having an effect like that of a strong medicine. Page 39.

dowager: a woman who holds some title, property or money from her deceased husband. Page 7.

down-to-earth: practical and realistic. Page 69.

drank deep: took into the mind or experienced (something) in depth, likened to the eager delight of one who satisfies physical thirst with a large quantity of liquid. Page 26.

dread: regarded with a feeling of respect mixed with fear or wonder. Page 26.

dreary: dull and uninteresting; tiresome. Page 81.

drifts: masses or banks of snow piled up by the wind. Page 22.

drives, four: the urge, thrust and purpose of life—SURVIVE!—in its four manifestations: self, sex, group and Mankind. Page 56.

droll: amusingly odd or comical. Page 114.

drug stores: stores selling medicines and a variety of other goods, including cosmetics, paperback books, magazines, stationery, cigarettes, etc., and sometimes serving soft drinks and light meals. Page 17.

due time, in: after the expected, appropriate or proper length of time. Page 80.

dug: living or residing, especially temporarily. Page 22.

dullars: a spelling that represents an informal pronunciation of the word *dollars.* Page 117.

dumbfounded: speechless with amazement; astonished. Page 79.

dwindling ratio: a *ratio* is a corresponding relationship between two different things; proportional relation. *Dwindling* means becoming less in any way. Here, the *dwindling ratio* shows that the less tired the person is, the less pain he will experience. Page 29.

dynamic: 1. the urge, thrust and purpose of life—SURVIVE!—in its four manifestations: self, sex, group and Mankind. Page 2.

2. the tenacity to life and vigor and persistence in survival. *Tenacity* is the quality of continuing steadily, keeping a firm hold on; toughness. Page 44.

E

earth-shaking: extremely great or important or having an extremely powerful effect. Page 38.

East: the countries of eastern Asia, especially China, Japan and their neighbors. Page 80.

East, the: the eastern United States, particularly with reference to the northeastern part of the country. Page 8.

Educational Dianetics: a branch of Dianetics that contains the body of organized knowledge necessary to train minds to their optimum efficiency and to an optimum of skill and knowledge in the various branches of the works of Man. Page 39.

eear, chawin' the: a spelling that represents an informal pronunciation of *chewing the ear*, talking to someone energetically or at length. Page 117.

eepistle: a playful spelling of *epistle* (emphasizing its first syllable), a formal term for a letter, especially a long, formal, instructive letter. Page 51.

effect: bring about; accomplish; make happen. Page 59.

efficacy: the capacity for producing a desired result or effect; effectiveness. Page 56.

80 and 85 over 40 to 50: low blood pressure. *80 and 85* refers to the measurement of blood pressure when the heart contracts to empty its blood into the circulatory system and *40 to 50* refers to the measurement of blood pressure when the heart relaxes and fills with blood. An adult's blood pressure is considered normal if it is in the range of 120 over 80. Abnormally low blood pressure may be caused by shock, malnutrition or some other disease or injury. Page 74.

El Cajon: a suburb of San Diego, a seaport in southwestern California. Page 17.

electrifying: causing a sense of thrilling excitement. Page 38.

electroconvulsive therapy: the psychiatric "treatment" of electric shock, a barbaric procedure wherein an electric current is applied to the person through electrodes placed on the head. It causes a severe convulsion (uncontrollable shaking of the body) or seizure (unconsciousness and inability to control movements of the body) and results in memory loss and permanent physical damage, leaving the person an emotional vegetable. Page 105.

elevate: raise to a higher moral, cultural or intellectual level. Page 80.

Elizabeth, New Jersey: a city in northeastern New Jersey, a state on the Atlantic coast of the United States. Elizabeth was the location of the first Hubbard Dianetic Research Foundation, 1950–1951. Page 1.

elucidated: made clear, explained. Page 32.

eluded: escaped perception or understanding of. Page 71.

eminent: standing above others in some quality or position; high in public estimation. Page 32.

emotionalism: a tendency to regard things emotionally or to respond emotionally as opposed to rationally. Page 43.

encysted: enclosed or encapsulated in, or as if in, a resistant covering. From *en,* to bring or put into a certain state or condition, and *cyst,* a closed, protective sac. Page 7.

endocrinological: of or having to do with *endocrinology,* the branch of biology dealing with the endocrine glands and their secretions. The endocrine glands secrete chemical substances in the body that regulate growth, development and function of certain tissues and coordinate many processes within the body. Page 15.

endowment: a gift of money or property so as to provide an income for the support of. Page 89.

energy, carry on their own: sustain the weight or burden of, by means of one's vital impulse or life force. Page 44.

enforgerated: a humorous form of *forged,* copied illegally so as to look genuine, usually for financial gain. Page 117.

engram: a moment of "unconsciousness" containing physical pain or painful emotion and all perceptions and is not available to the analytical mind (conscious, aware mind) as experience. Page 28.

engrossed: having one's attention completely occupied with. Page 44.

enjoin: command somebody with authority and emphasis to do something or behave in a certain way. Page 116.

enlightened: those that are free of ignorance, prejudice or superstition; individuals who are rational, tolerant and well-informed. Page 44.

en masse: a French phrase meaning as a group; all together. Page 34.

entertained: gave attention or consideration to. Page 26.

eon: any period of time in history or in the development of Man, especially with reference to cultural evolution; a time long since past. Page 100.

epilepsy, post-traumatic: a form of epilepsy following or resulting from trauma (physical injury). *Epilepsy* is a disorder of the nervous system that briefly interrupts the normal electrical activity of the brain, resulting in seizures and characterized by a variety of symptoms, including uncontrolled movements of the body, disorientation or confusion, sudden fear or loss of consciousness. Page 66.

epistle: a formal term for a letter, especially a long, formal, instructive letter. Page 116.

equitable: of actions, arrangements, decisions, etc., that is fair to all concerned; just. Page 80.

equity: a claim or interest, as to a property. Page 113.

et al.: abbreviation for the Latin phrase *et alia,* meaning "and others." Page 98.

ethnological: of or having to do with *ethnology,* the science that analyzes cultures, especially in regard to their historical development and the similarities and dissimilarities between them. Page 26.

euphemistically: in a manner that substitutes a mild, indirect or vague expression for one thought to be offensive, harsh or blunt. Page 106.

Evolution of a Science: one of the first publications about Dianetics, which appeared in the May 1950 issue of *Astounding Science Fiction* magazine. L. Ron Hubbard's description of how he came to make the breakthrough discoveries of Dianetics was later released as the book *Dianetics: The Evolution of a Science.* Page 16.

exact scientist: somebody who has scientific training or works in one of the *exact sciences,* subjects in which facts can be accurately observed and results can be accurately predicted. Page 43.

"Excalibur": a philosophic manuscript written by L. Ron Hubbard in 1938. Although unpublished as such, the body of information it contained has since been released in various Dianetics and Scientology materials. (*Excalibur* was the name of the magic sword of King Arthur, legendary British hero, said to have ruled in the fifth or sixth century A.D.). Page 17.

expansive: communicative about a wide or comprehensive range of data or information. Page 27.

expended: used or spent. Page 81.

exploits: acts remarkable for brilliance or daring. Page 26.

Explorers Club: an organization, headquartered in New York and founded in 1904, devoted exclusively to promoting the science of exploration. To further this aim, it provides grants for those who wish to participate in field research projects and expeditions. It has provided logistical support for some of the twentieth century's most daring expeditions. L. Ron Hubbard was a lifetime member of the Explorers Club. Page 2.

Explorers Journal, The: a quarterly periodical published since 1921 by the *Explorers Club,* an organization, headquartered in New York and founded in 1904, devoted exclusively to promoting the science of exploration. The club's *Journal* publishes articles and photographs from club members and others on expeditions across the globe. Page 2.

expressly: for the particular or specific purpose; specially. Page 105.

exquisite: extreme or intense. Page vii.

extant: in existence. Page 63.

eye of (that, the) storm: the calm area at the center of a storm or hurricane, around which winds of high velocity move. Used figuratively. Page 1.

F

fabricated: made up or invented without basis in fact. Page 113.

far country: literally, a place at a great distance. Also used figuratively for an area of activity that is distant, advanced or the like. Page 26.

ferocity: the state or quality of being hostile or violent, like a wild animal. Page 94.

file clerk: a system in the mind that hands out data when asked for it. The file clerk operates like a selector and feeder device in a computer. When a computer wants data, such a device gets it from the memory storage areas and gives it out. Page 72.

fireball: something that resembles a ball of fire, such as a roundish area of extreme inflammation. Page 8.

first class: first, highest or best group in a system of classification. Page 80.

flailing: striking or attacking (something) in a violent, uncontrollable manner, as if by swinging the arms around wildly. Page 108.

flak-shredded: torn or cut into strips or pieces (figuratively speaking) by antiaircraft fire. *Flak* is antiaircraft fire directed from the ground, especially as experienced by the crews of combat airplanes at which the fire is directed. Page 38.

flank speed: the maximum possible speed of a ship. Page 54.

flawed: having imperfections or shortcomings; defective; faulty. Page 16.

flurry: a number of things arriving suddenly and simultaneously; a burst of activity. Page 50.

folds up: breaks down; collapses; fails. Page 43.

folic acid: a B vitamin found in leafy green vegetables, citrus fruits, cereals, beans, poultry and egg yolk and important in the formation of red blood cells. Also known as *vitamin B_9*. Page 74.

foolhardy: showing boldness or courage but not wisdom or good sense. Page 89.

Ford Foundation: a privately owned institution founded by contributions from American automobile manufacturers Henry Ford (1863–1947) and his son Edsel Ford (1893–1943). The foundation issues grants for experimental, developmental or other projects, in such fields as behavioral sciences (such as psychology), economics and administration. Since its inception it has granted billions of dollars to fund such activities. Page 89.

forecast: predicted as a future condition or occurrence. Page 41.

fork in the road, at a: at a point where one must make a decision or choice between two things. A *fork* is a point in a road or river where it splits into two or more branches. Page 56.

formality: a procedure that must be followed because it is a rule or requirement but which has little significance in itself. Page 113.

Forrestal: James Vincent Forrestal (1892–1949), American banker and government official. During World War II (1939–1945) he held a high position in the administration of the US Navy and in 1947 he was appointed as the country's first secretary of defense, in charge of all US military forces, from which position he initiated a reorganization and coordination of the US armed services. In March 1949 Forrestal resigned his post due to what doctors called "depression" and shortly thereafter was admitted to the Bethesda Naval Medical Center in Maryland, where he was treated by psychiatrists. In May he committed suicide by jumping out of a hospital window. *See also* **Raines, George N.** Page 100.

fortified: made more effective, as with additions designed to improve performance. Page 39.

Fortune: a business magazine founded in 1930 and focusing on topics in business, the economy and social issues connected with the world of business. *Fortune* is one of more than one hundred magazines published by *Time, Inc.,* the publishing company that also produces *Time* magazine. Page 54.

4 bells: *bell* is a nautical term meaning any of the half-hour units of time rung on the bell of a ship during a *watch,* a four-hour period of time during which assigned personnel of the ship are on duty. The first watch is midnight to 4 A.M. and during this watch, one bell indicates 12:30 A.M., two bells indicate 1:00 A.M., three bells indicate 1:30 A.M. and four bells indicate 2 A.M. Page 52.

Four Humors: the four basic fluids of the body earlier regarded as determining, by their relative proportions, a person's disposition and physical characteristics. For example, one of the humors was blood, which was regarded as bringing about cheerfulness and a strong body. Another humor, found in the digestive area of the body, was thought to cause gloominess. Page 39.

fraction: a small or tiny part, amount or proportion. Page vii.

frame of reference: a set of concepts, values, customs, views, etc., by means of which an individual or group perceives or evaluates data, communicates ideas and regulates behavior. Page 42.

freelancing: writing stories or articles for a number of employers rather than working on a regular salary basis for one employer. Page 56.

French Morocco: a portion of present-day Morocco, a kingdom located in northwestern Africa that was controlled by France and Spain between 1912 and 1956. Page 38.

Freud: Sigmund Freud (1856–1939), Austrian founder of psychoanalysis who emphasized that unconscious memories of a sexual nature control a person's behavior. Page 17.

frowned on: looked at with strong disapproval or dislike, especially on moral or ethical grounds. Page 117.

fruition: a state or point in which something had a desired outcome or produced the results intended or hoped for. Page 49.

full-fledged: with or having full rank, standing or status. Page 72.

full-scale: complete or to the utmost limit; involving all possible means, facilities, etc. Page 24.

FW-190: the Focke-Wulf FW-190, a single-seat, single-engine German fighter aircraft designed in the late 1930s and used during World War II (1939–1945). With over twenty thousand produced throughout the war, the FW-190 was one of the best fighter aircraft of the time. Page 38.

G

Gainesville: a city in northern Florida, a southeastern state in the United States. Page 75.

gal: a girl or woman. Page 63.

galaxies: large systems of stars, each of which is held together by gravitation and isolated from similar systems by vast regions of space. Page 34.

galley(s): in early forms of printing, a trial copy of some printed work made from metal type placed in a shallow tray of brass or wood (called a *galley*). The metal type was locked in place so a *proof,* or printed sample, could be made to check for any errors. It was usually one single column with wide margins for noting corrections. Page 52.

gangrenous: affected by *gangrene,* death and decay of body tissue often occurring in a limb, caused by insufficient blood supply and usually following injury or disease. Page 7.

gauntlet, threw down the: issued a challenge, from the custom during the Middle Ages of throwing down a glove or gauntlet in challenging an opponent. A *gauntlet* is a glove with a long wide cuff that covers part of the forearm, made of fabric, leather or, in the past, metal, when worn as part of armor. Page 106.

general delivery: a mail-delivery service or a department of a post office that handles the delivery of mail at a post office window to persons who do not have any permanent street address or who for other reasons call for their mail without waiting for carrier service. Often used as an address. Page 17.

general semantics: a philosophical approach to language, developed by Alfred Korzybski (1879–1950), which sought a scientific basis for a clear understanding of the difference between words and reality and the ways in which words themselves can influence and limit Man's ability to think. Korzybski believed that men unthinkingly identify words with the objects they represent and have nonoptimum reactions to words based on past experiences. He also developed a highly organized system of the different categories of perceptions (called sensations) and created a precise table displaying their various physical characteristics and properties. Page 29.

generative: concerned with being the point of origin or creation of something. Page 27.

germane: closely or significantly related; pertinent. Page 3.

Gerontological Society: a nonprofit healthcare organization that promotes research in aging and disseminates information to researchers, educators, practitioners and to decision- and opinion-makers. *Gerontology* is the scientific study of the process of aging and of the problems associated with old age. Page 16.

Gestalten schools: systems of therapy using *Gestalt psychology,* a branch of psychology based on the belief that experience is a unified pattern and is more than the sum of its smaller, independent events. (*Gestalten* is the plural of *Gestalt,* the German word for pattern, form or shape.) According to this psychology, when healthy persons are confronted with various elements, they perceive a whole pattern rather than bits and pieces and therefore respond appropriately. Unhealthy persons perceive and respond to a bit or a piece. Gestalt therapy seeks to remedy the inability to respond appropriately. Page 1.

ghosted: performed as a *ghost writer*, a person who writes speeches, books, articles, etc., for another person, the latter being named as the author and taking the credit for it. Page 56.

Ginny: Virginia Heinlein (1916–2003), wife of author Robert A. Heinlein. Page 52.

gits: a spelling that represents an informal pronunciation of the word *gets*. The phrase "them as has, *gits*" means that those people who have something tend to get more. Page 44.

Gladwyne, Pennsylvania: a community in southeastern Pennsylvania, a state in the eastern United States. Page 63.

glaring(ly): very easily seen or detected. Page 71.

glimmer: a faint glimpse or idea (of knowledge, hope, etc.); a faint perception. Page 58.

God-given right: a claim or the freedom to do something existing as part of the natural order of the universe rather than arranged by humanity. Page 43.

golden age: the most flourishing period in the history of something; the time of highest achievement or greatest development. Page 34.

golly: a word used to express surprise, shock or dismay, or as a mild oath; often in phrases such as *my golly* or *by golly*. Page 118.

grand: great in extent, magnitude, value, importance or consequence. (*Grand* refers to an offense that involves some feature defined by law that enhances a crime, such as the intention of the criminal or the special vulnerability of the victim, and therefore warrants a higher sentence.) Page 117.

grand larceny: the unlawful taking and removing of another's personal property with the intent of permanently depriving the owner, when the value is large (grand), being above a certain amount specified by law. Page 117.

grapevine: a person-to-person method of spreading rumors, gossip, information, etc., by informal or unofficial conversation, letter writing or the like. Page 85.

grass roots: common or ordinary people. Page 70.

gratifying: giving pleasure or satisfaction; pleasing. Page 41.

gripped: held firmly; seized tightly; under the control of. Used figuratively. Page 81.

groping: searching for something hesitantly or with uncertainty. Page 57.

ground: a foundation or basis on which knowledge, belief or opinion rests. Page 90.

grounds that, on the: with the excuse or justification that; with something asserted as a basis or reason. Page 42.

Guild Theatre: a hall in Los Angeles, California, where L. Ron Hubbard delivered lectures on the subject of Dianetics technology applied to groups. Page 76.

guinea pig: someone who agrees to be the subject of a test or trial. Literally, a *guinea pig* is a plump, short-eared, furry domesticated animal, native to South America, widely kept as a pet and used as a subject in scientific experiments. Page 97.

gulf: a gap that serves as a means of separation; a wide interval. Page 44.

H

hacked: cut with heavy blows in an irregular or random fashion. Used figuratively. Page 26.

hadda: a spelling that represents an informal pronunciation of *had to,* meaning must. Page 116.

had (someone): placed or maneuvered (someone) into a defenseless or vulnerable position or a position bringing certain defeat. Page 116.

hallucination: false or distorted perception of objects or events with a compelling sense of their reality. Page 31.

halo effect: a phenomena that occurs with one's vision where one sees a halo (bright or dark ring of light) around visible light sources. Page 73.

hamlet: a group of houses or a small village in the country. Page 71.

hand, to: near or close by; easily available and ready to be used. Page 80.

haphazard: characterized by lack of order or planning, or any obvious principle of organization; random. Page 1.

hard by: close by; very near. Page 27.

hat(s), under (one's): private, secret or confidential. Page 86.

haul forth: pull or drag out, using effort or force. Page 28.

heartfelt: deeply or sincerely felt; genuine. Page 62.

heeling: (of the deck of a ship) tilting, as when a ship, pushed by wind or waves, leans to one side. Page 52.

heell: a spelling that represents a humorous pronunciation of the word *hell.* Page 51.

Heinlein, Robert: Robert "Bob" Heinlein (1907–1988), an American author considered one of the most important writers of science fiction. Emerging during science fiction's Golden Age (1939–1949), Heinlein went on to write many novels, including the classic *Stranger in a Strange Land* (1961). He won four Hugo Awards and was presented with the first Grand Master Nebula Award for lifetime achievement in science fiction. Page 3.

Hell's Kitchen: in New York City, a nickname for a part of the west side of Manhattan, so called from the slums and crime in parts of this area during the 1800s and early 1900s. Page 7.

helm, at the: in a position of control or of highest executive power (as in an organization). Page 26.

hereditary: (of a characteristic or disease) able to be passed on from parents to their offspring or descendants. Page 35.

Hermitage House: a publishing firm in New York City, New York, founded in 1947 by editor and publisher Arthur Ceppos (1910–1997). In May 1950, Hermitage House was the first to publish *Dianetics: The Modern Science of Mental Health.* Page 24.

heuristic: using experimentation, evaluation or trial-and-error methods; involving investigation and conclusions based on invariable workability. Page 27.

hinges, knocked (one) off (one's): unexpectedly caused one to feel destabilized, as through bewilderment or shock. Literally, a hinge is the jointed device on which a door, gate, lid, etc., swings or moves, thus allowing it to function. Page 17.

hitch: a (unexpected) difficulty, problem or obstacle in the way of progress. Page 63.

hi-tension: *tension* in this sense is a synonym for *voltage,* the amount of pressure or force behind an electrical flow. *Hi* is a shortening of *high. Hi-tension wires* are electrical power lines designed for carrying large amounts of voltage, usually found well off the ground, strung across a series of poles, one after another. Page 38.

hither and yon: in this direction and in that (alternately); to and fro; in various directions. Page 50.

hitherto: up to this time; until now. Page 1.

holdover: a thing that remains from a previous period. Page 100.

hole: a position from which it is difficult to escape; a mess. Page 59.

holistic: relating to or concerned with wholes or with complete systems rather than with the analysis of, treatment of or dissection into parts. Page 32.

Homo Novis: new man; from the Latin words *homo,* man, and *novus,* new. Page 54.

homonymic: of or characteristic of a *homonym,* a word that is spelled or pronounced in the same way as one or more other words but has a different meaning: *rowed* and *road* are homonyms. Page 80.

honing: bringing to a state of increased excellence or completion, especially over a period of time. From the idea of rubbing or sharpening on a *hone,* a special stone used for sharpening instruments that require a fine edge, such as razors or knives. Page 2.

hooman: a spelling that represents an informal pronunciation of the word *human.* Page 17.

horizon: the limit or extent of one's outlook, experience, interest, knowledge, etc.; literally, the line or circle that forms the apparent boundary between Earth and sky. Page 26.

hormone-therapy: the treatment of disease or disorders by administering hormones. *Hormones* are chemical substances secreted by glands or tissues in the body that regulate growth and development, control the function of various tissues, support reproductive functions and regulate metabolism (the process used to break down food to create energy). Page 20.

hot: prompting intense discussion or debate. Page 17.

humanities: branches of learning concerned with human thought and relations, as distinguished from the sciences; especially literature, philosophy, history, etc. (Originally, *the humanities* referred to education that would enable a person to freely think and judge for himself, as opposed to a narrow study of technical skills.) Page 107.

hypnoanalysis: a method of psychoanalysis in which a patient is hypnotized in an attempt to reach analytic data and early emotional reactions. Page 30.

hypochondriac: one who suffers an excessive anxiety over his health, often with imaginary illnesses. Page 17.

I

ill: hardly at all; with difficulty or inconvenience. Page 57.

illuminating: informative and enlightening, often by revealing or emphasizing facts that were previously unknown. Page vii.

immunity: exemption or protection from something unpleasant, such as a duty or penalty, to which others are subject. Page 108.

impassioned: filled with or expressing strong feelings. Page 50.

impetus: a driving or impelling force. Page 82.

imposed upon: forced upon, as something to be endured. Page 65.

inaccessible: unapproachable; unable to gain access to an engram. Page 92.

inasmuch as: to the extent or degree, as far as. Page 69.

incidence: the rate of occurrence of something, especially of something unwanted. Page 32.

inciting: urging or persuading to act in a certain way; provoking action by somebody. Page 108.

indelible: that cannot be eliminated, erased, etc.; permanent. Page 35.

indict: a playful spelling of *indite,* express in writing; write down. Page 51.

indifferent: rather poor or bad; not good at all. Page 39.

indomitable: that cannot be subdued or overcome, such as persons, will, courage or spirit; unconquerable. Page 17.

induced: 1. brought about, produced or caused. Page 19.

2. led or moved by persuasion, as to some action or state of mind. Page 19.

indulge: give in to or yield to (an urge, desire, etc.); allow or permit to happen or exist. Page 81.

indulging: engaging or taking part in, often with the idea of freely or eagerly doing so. Page 107.

Industrial Dianetics: a branch of Dianetics containing the body of knowledge necessary to improve to its highest levels the world of *industry,* those companies that manufacture or sell products made from raw materials, as opposed to products that are grown and then sold. Page 39.

inferiority complex(es): a term used to describe a mental obsession with the idea of being *inferior,* of less importance, value or worth. Page 17.

infiltrate: penetrate a group gradually or secretly with the intention of doing harm or seizing control from within. Page 105.

Infinite Mind: the theory or belief that there is an absolute mind, the mind of the All, being present everywhere and independent of time and space; the source and foundation of existence, possessed of all possible power, wisdom and excellence, sometimes said in reference to God. Page 42.

in for it: about to experience certain consequences, possibly not entirely to one's liking, especially on account of one's own actions. Page 63.

injunction: command, order or authoritative warning. Page 21.

insofar: to such a degree or extent. Page 99.

intellect: capacity for thinking and acquiring knowledge, especially of a high or complex order; mental capacity. Page 80.

interim: an interval of time between one event, process or period and another. Page 40.

interlinked: connected together; (something) being associated or related (to something else) in several ways. Page 105.

interment: the burial of a dead body as in a grave or tomb. Page 38.

interminably: in a seemingly endless manner; without end or limit; endlessly. Page 49.

in toto: in its entirety or as a whole. Page 57.

introspection: the detailed mental examination of one's own feelings, thoughts and motives. Page 1.

inverse ratio: the ratio (proportionate relationship) of two quantities that vary inversely (inverse is opposite to or reversing something); that is, one increases in the exact proportion as the other decreases. Page 88.

irascible: easily angered; quick-tempered. Page 3.

irrepressible: full of energy and enthusiasm; impossible to control or stop. Page 54.

Isles of Greece: the islands (isles), of which there are roughly two thousand, that belong to the country of Greece. Page 52.

ivy-covered walls: having the walls of buildings covered with *ivy,* a climbing vine whose leaves remain dark green all year. Used figuratively in reference to an educational institution, because the walls of many major colleges and universities are traditionally covered with ivy. Page 54.

J

jackal(s): somebody who works with others to deceive people, especially to swindle them out of money. Literally, a *jackal* is a wild dog of Asia and Africa that hunts during the night in packs and feeds on dead animals. Page 121.

jackpot: the highest prize in a game or contest, such as a large sum of money in a gambling game. *Hit the jackpot* means achieve a great or sudden success. Page 63.

Japan, still devastated: a reference to the state of Japan in 1950. At the end of World War II (1939–1945), one-quarter of its buildings lay in ashes due to repeated bombings of cities and atomic bombs dropped on the cities of Hiroshima and Nagasaki. Production was only one-third of its prewar level and it was not until 1955 that Japan's economy returned to its prewar levels. Page 78.

Jefferson: Thomas Jefferson (1743–1826), third president of the United States (1801–1809) and author of the Declaration of Independence (1776), which stated fundamental principles of human rights (including that all men "are endowed by their Creator with certain unalienable Rights, that among these are Life, Liberty and the pursuit of Happiness") and proclaimed the American colonies to be free and independent of England. Page 99.

jocularly: jokingly; humorously or playfully. Page 50.

Johns Hopkins: referring to Johns Hopkins Hospital, which shares a campus with Johns Hopkins University, located in Baltimore, Maryland. The university is known for research, teaching and patient care; the hospital conducts extensive medical research. Page 71.

Joisey: a spelling that represents a humorous pronunciation of the word *Jersey,* as in *New Jersey,* a state in the eastern United States, on the Atlantic coast, near New York. Page 52.

Judiciary Dianetics: Judiciary Dianetics covers the field of adjudication within the society and among the societies of Man. Of necessity, it embraces jurisprudence (the theory or philosophy of law) and its codes and establishes precision definitions and equations for the establishment of equity (fairness). It is the science of judgment. Page 76.

Jung: Carl Gustav Jung (1875–1961), Swiss psychiatrist. He disagreed with Freud's emphasis on sex as a driving force and instead theorized that all humans inherit what he termed a "collective unconscious" containing universal symbols and memories from their ancestral past, such as found in religions, myths and fairy tales. Page 25.

juvenile: childish or immature; considered as characteristic of someone not fully matured in intellect or behavior. Page 57.

K

kamikaze(s): during World War II (1939–1945), a member of a special corps in the Japanese Air Force charged with the suicidal mission of crashing an aircraft loaded with explosives into an enemy target, especially a warship. Page 27.

Kansas City: a city in western Missouri, a state in the central United States. Page 92.

keyed-in: literally, a *key* is a small manual device for opening, closing or switching electronic contacts. *Key-in* is used to describe an inactive engram that has started up and become active. Page 29.

knocking out: getting rid of; eliminating as if removing forcibly. Page 92.

Komazawa University: one of the oldest universities in Japan. It was established in 1592 and is located in the city of Tokyo. Page 79.

L

LA *Daily News*: a newspaper founded in Los Angeles, California, in the early 1920s, originally named the Los Angeles *Daily Illustrated News.* Though the paper had a large circulation through the 1940s, it gradually declined and ceased publication in 1954. Page 105.

large, at: as a whole; in general. Page 82.

last rites: rites (ceremonies) administered to a person who is about to die. Page 51.

later'n: later than. (The *'n* is an informal, reduced form of *than.*) Page 117.

latterly: at a subsequent time; later. Page 50.

laurel on the brow, wear: figuratively, achieve victory and receive a crown of *laurel,* a wreath made from the leaves of the *laurel plant,* a small evergreen tree native to lands near the Mediterranean Sea. In ancient times, laurel wreaths were used as a mark of honor or victory, for example, to crown the winners of athletic events. Page 54.

lay: nonprofessional. Page 109.

laymen: those who do not belong to some particular profession or who are not expert in some branch of knowledge or art. Page 107.

leading edge: the forward edge of an aircraft wing. On fighter aircraft, guns of various sizes were often mounted on the outer wing and also near the nose. Those near the nose were timed to fire through the rotating propeller blades. Page 38.

league: an association, as of people, groups or the like, with common interests or goals, that combine for mutual cooperation. Page 26.

Left Bank: part of the city of Paris lying south of the Seine River, a famous center of artist and student life. Page 7.

letter slot: a long, narrow opening in a door or in a wall near the entrance of a building, through which letters, etc., are delivered. Page 117.

liability: disadvantage or something that is likely to cause problems. Page 29.

libel: the action of publishing false and malicious statements about someone. Page 117.

Life: the name of a weekly American picture magazine, introduced in 1936 by the publisher of *Time* magazine, Henry Luce (1898–1967). Page 105.

lightly: with indifference or unconcern; carelessly; thoughtlessly. Page 57.

linear descendant: a thing that comes directly from something that existed previously. *Linear* describes a direct or clear relationship between two things. A *descendant* is something derived in function or general character from an earlier form. Page 105.

liver extract: a dry brownish powder that comes from animal liver, most commonly from cattle. Liver extract is used to make medicine, as it is capable of stimulating the production of red blood cells. It is used for increasing liver function, treating chronic liver diseases and preventing liver damage, as well as enhancing muscle development and improving strength. Page 74.

Livingstone: David Livingstone (1813–1873), Scottish missionary and physician. For more than thirty years he explored southern and central Africa, covering one-third of the continent while attempting to find a trade route into the heart of Africa. He was the first European to see the Zambezi River falls (which he named Victoria Falls after the Queen of England) and the first European to cross the full width of southern Africa. His explorations revealed that the interior of the African continent was not dry wasteland, as many nineteenth-century geographers believed. Page 27.

lock(s): an analytical moment in which the perceptics of the engram are approximated, thus restimulating the engram or bringing it into action, the present time perceptics being erroneously interpreted by the reactive mind to mean that the same condition which produced physical pain once before is now again at hand. Page 92.

lodged: made a formal complaint or appeal by handing the documents to the appropriate authority. Page 50.

log: a record of progress or occurrences, as on an expedition or other journey. Page 29.

long sea: an expanse of water over which a ship or boat sails, characterized by a uniform, steady motion of long and extensive waves. As contrasted with a *short sea,* one having irregular, broken waves that tend to break over the side of the ship. Page 52.

longshoreman: a person who works along the shore, in the docks, loading and unloading ships. Page 7.

loose, turn: make free; release. Page 117.

lopsided: uneven; not balanced due to one side being heavier, larger or stronger than the other. Used figuratively. Page 107.

lore: accumulated facts, traditions or beliefs about a particular subject. Page 39.

low reality case: an individual who has a low sense of reality and is out of contact with it and with the universe around him. This individual has a hard time believing his own data or having confidence in data that he brings up about his past. Page 92.

Lucretius: (ca. 98–55 B.C.) Roman poet who was the author of the unfinished instructional poem *On the Nature of Things,* published in six books, which sets forth in outline a complete science of the universe. The poem includes an explanation of the stages of life on Earth and the origin and development of civilization, as well as ideas on evolution and the production, distribution and extinction of various life forms, similar to the principle of evolution given in early Indian (Eastern) writings. Page 99.

lunge (of the heart): a *lunge* is a forceful and often abrupt movement or action; a surge. Used here in reference to a phenomenon that occurs in childbirth wherein, once the umbilical cord is cut, the baby has to start breathing, as his heart is no longer able to pump and obtain oxygenated blood from the mother. Page 20.

M

mainstay: a thing that acts as a chief support or part. Page 34.

make-believe: of or like imaginary situations or events that somebody, especially a child playing, pretends are true; of or like a fantasy. Page 57.

malaria: an infectious disease transmitted by the bite of infected mosquitoes. Common in hot countries, the disease is characterized by recurring chills and fever. During the wars of the twentieth century, more soldiers were lost to malaria than to bullets. Page 27.

Manhattan: one of the five sections that make up New York City. Located on Manhattan Island, it is the main economic center of the city. Page 7.

manic: characterized by abnormal excitability, exaggerated feeling of well-being, etc. Page 29.

martyr: somebody who makes sacrifices or suffers greatly to advance a cause or principle. Page 97.

massed: brought together in large numbers; assembled. Page 38.

Mathieu, Hubert: Hubert "Matty" Mathieu (1897–1954), American painter, sculptor, illustrator, lecturer and writer. Mathieu created a wide variety of art and was well known for producing illustrations for magazines and newspapers, as well as for his portraits. Page 7.

May *Journal*: a reference to the May 1950 issue of *Ladies Home Journal,* one of America's leading magazines in the twentieth century, in which Mrs. Byall's article on helping the handicapped appeared. Page 64.

Mayne: Edna Mayne van Vogt (1905–1975), Canadian-born science fiction writer whose stories were published under the name E. Mayne Hull. She was the first wife of Alfred Elton van Vogt. Page 85.

Mayo's: a reference to the *Mayo Clinic,* a large medical clinic established in 1889 by English-born American doctor and surgeon William W. Mayo (1819–1911), in Rochester, Minnesota, USA. The clinic originally specialized in surgery but expanded to deliver other medical services. Page 66.

May, Rollo: (1909–1994) American psychologist and writer, author of a derogatory article on *Dianetics: The Modern Science of Mental Health* in the newspaper the *New York Times.* Page 106.

Md.: an abbreviation for *Maryland,* an eastern state of the United States. Page 19.

MD: abbreviation of Latin *Medicinae Doctor,* Doctor of Medicine; a physician. Page 72.

medicine drumming: a reference to the beating of a *medicine drum,* a drum used by primitive medicine men to cure illnesses by driving evil spirits out of an ill person. Page 30.

medico: an informal term for a medical practitioner, such as a doctor. Page 95.

memoranda: plural of *memorandum,* an informal message written for circulation within a company, concerning company business. Page 49.

Menninger Clinic: a psychiatric clinic and training facility located in Topeka, Kansas, USA, founded by American psychiatrist, Karl Menninger (1893–1990) and his father. Page 106.

Metropolitan Life Tower: a 700-foot tall (213 meters), fifty-story skyscraper in New York City, built between 1893 and 1909 and serving as the world headquarters of the Metropolitan Life Insurance Company, a US insurance firm founded in the mid-1860s. Page 54.

Middle Ages: the period in European history between ancient and more modern times. This is considered to be from the fifth century, at the end of the Roman Empire, and the early fifteenth century, a point when major cultural and artistic changes began occurring. Page 39.

midflight: in the middle of a course of action or train of thought. Page 42.

mighty: an informal term used chiefly in North America to mean extremely or to a great degree; very. Page 117.

military-industrial complex: a network of a nation's military force together with all of the industries that support it. Page 106.

mire: thick, slimy and often deep mud, as that found in a swamp. Page 81.

misadventures: unfortunate events or instances of bad luck. Page 31.

misc biz: a shortening of *miscellaneous business,* matters or affairs consisting of many different things or kinds of things that have no necessary connection with each other. Page 85.

misconstrue: misunderstand as to the meaning; take in the wrong sense. Page 81.

misdemeanor: a minor criminal offense. Page 119.

monkey out of, make a: cause (someone) to look foolish or stupid. Page 17.

monopoly: an organization or group that has an exclusive possession or control of something. Page 105.

monotony: a state of utter sameness that provides no challenge, interest or insight; tedious sameness. Page 81.

Morgan, Parker: a board member of an early Dianetics organization. Page 85.

moronic: mentally retarded; of a *moron,* a former term describing someone with significant learning difficulties and impaired social skills, having an intelligence quotient (IQ) from 50 to 69. Page 43.

mortgage: an agreement by which someone borrows money from an organization, as in order to purchase something involving a large expense, such as a house. As a guarantee that the loan will be paid back, the borrower promises that the lender can take possession of property (usually land, buildings, etc.) owned by the borrower if he fails to pay the money back. *Mortgage* is from earlier French words *mort,* dead, and *gage,* pledge or promise, because property pledged is lost if the loan is not repaid. Used humorously. Page 119.

mothballs, in: in storage or reserve. Literally, *mothballs* are small, chemically treated balls that repel moths from clothes that are in storage. Page 17.

mounted: prepared and launched, as an attack or a campaign. Page 105.

Mrs. Swilch: a made-up name. Page 54.

ms(s): an abbreviation for *manuscript* (and *mss,* the abbreviation for the plural), a written or typewritten text, such as one being prepared for, or awaiting, publication. Page 52.

mundane: common or ordinary. Page 8.

mystic: of obscure or mysterious character or significance. Page 66.

mysticism: the belief that it is possible to achieve knowledge of spiritual truths and God through contemplation or through deep and careful thought. Page 35.

N

narcosynthesis: hypnotism brought about by drugs. Page 15.

national columnist: a person who writes or prepares a column (a series of feature articles regularly appearing in a newspaper or magazine by a particular writer or about a certain subject) for a newspaper or magazine for an entire nation. Page 49.

natural laws: principles or bodies of laws considered as coming from correct reasoning and observations of nature. Page 27.

Naval Medical Institute: the *National Naval Medical Center,* also known as *Bethesda Naval Hospital,* one of the largest military medical centers in the United States. Founded in the early

1940s, the center originally consisted of a hospital, medical and dental schools and the Naval Medical Research Institute. It is run by the United States Navy. Page 105.

navy yard: a navy-owned *shipyard,* a place where warships are built and repaired. Page 95.

Nazi: of or about the National Socialist German Workers' party, which in 1933, under Adolf Hitler, seized political control of the country, suppressing all opposition and establishing a dictatorship over all activities of the people. It promoted and enforced the belief that the German people were superior and that the Jews were inferior (and thus were to be eliminated). The party was officially abolished in 1945 at the conclusion of World War II (1939–1945). *Nazi* is from the first part of the German word for the name of the party, *Nati(onalsozialistische),* which is pronounced *nazi* in German. Page 105.

Nazi experimentation: a reference to the practice of conducting medical experiments on prisoners in Nazi Germany concentration camps during World War II (1939–1945). *Concentration camps* were a type of prison camp established for the confinement and persecution of Jews, political opponents, religious dissenters, etc. In such camps, along with the mass extermination of prisoners, thousands of persons were subjected to inhuman and highly abusive "medical" experiments. *See also* **Nazi.** Page 105.

ne'er-do-well: a worthless fellow who is idle, ineffective and irresponsible. *Ne'er* is short for *never.* Page 57.

netherworld: literally, the *underworld,* any region lying or viewed as lying below the ordinary one. Page 2.

neurasthenia: a condition marked by fatigue, irritability, weakness, anxiety, etc. Page 74.

New Jersey: a state in the eastern United States, on the Atlantic coast, near New York. Page 3.

news service: an agency that gathers and distributes information about current events. Page 54.

New York State Commission against Discrimination: the commission (group of persons authoritatively charged with particular functions) in the state of New York formed to investigate and reconcile complaints of discrimination in employment practices. In the early 1950s, New York was one of seven states in the United States having laws that included a means of enforcing nondiscriminatory practices in employment. Page 56.

New York Times: a daily newspaper established in 1851 and published in New York City, New York. Its Sunday edition includes book reviews and the prestigious *New York Times* bestseller list. Page 49.

nil: zero; so small as not to be measurable. Page 58.

nomenclature: a system or set of names or designations used in a particular field. Page 2.

nominal: named as a mere matter of form, being very small; minimal. Page 106.

nominally: being such in name only, not in fact. Page 88.

nonauthoritarian: free from enforced, unquestioning obedience to an authority, thereby allowing individual freedom of judgment, decision or action. Page 100.

note: a *promissory note,* a written promise to pay a certain sum of money to a certain person by a specified date. Page 116.

nucleus: a central part about which other parts are grouped or gathered; core. Page 89.

null: amounting to nothing; without effect or consequence. Page 32.

number on, have one's: (of a bullet or shell) be thought of as that which will bring about a person's death. Page 38.

number seven key: an analogy made by LRH between the reactive mind and an adding machine in which the number seven key has been held down so that it is always added into every computation. Of course it cannot compute correctly or get correct answers from data as long as this condition exists. Page 57.

nuts to crack, hardest: the most difficult people to make understand or do something. Page 72.

nutty: strange, foolish or crazy. Page 17.

NY: an abbreviation for *New York,* a city and major port in southeastern New York State, a state in the eastern United States. Page 51.

NY Times: an abbreviation for *New York Times. See also* **New York Times.** Page 51.

O

Oak Knoll Naval Hospital: a naval hospital located in Oakland, California, USA, where LRH spent time recovering from injuries sustained during World War II (1939–1945) and researching the effect of the mind on the physical recovery of patients. Page 15.

obviate: do away with or prevent by effective measures. Page 28.

Ochsner Clinic: a medical facility established in 1942 in uptown New Orleans, now expanded to the Ochsner Health System, with numerous hospitals in southeastern Louisiana. Founder Alton Ochsner (1896–1981) was a pioneer in exposing the hazards of tobacco and its link to lung cancer. Page 71.

ocular: of or pertaining to the eyes. Page 73.

offhand: casual; informal. Page 49.

Ohio: a state in the north central United States. Page 38.

oilman: a person who owns or operates oil wells or an executive in the petroleum industry. Page 113.

onslaught: an attack; especially a vigorous or destructive assault or attack. Page 3.

on-the-scene: done at the site of an action or event. Page 7.

oodles: an informal term for a large quantity. Page 85.

opened (case): gotten (something or someone) going; begun the operation of. Page 45.

open letter: a published letter on a subject of general interest, usually addressed to an individual but intended for general readership. Page 34.

opinionation: the act of giving one's opinion, judgment or viewpoint on something, especially when biased or unreasonable. Page 107.

oppressed: prevented from having opportunities and freedom by cruel and unfair use of force or authority. Page 81.

optometrist: a specialist in *optometry,* the practice or profession of examining the eyes for defects in vision and eye disorders in order to prescribe corrective lenses or other appropriate treatment. Also called an eye doctor. Page 74.

organic: relating to or affecting organs or an organ of the body. Page 35.

organic sensations: senses which tell the nervous system the state of the various organs of the body. Page 28.

Orient: the countries of eastern Asia, especially China, Japan and their neighbors. Page 78.

overboard, going: doing something to an extreme degree; going too far in some action. Page 63.

overextended: stretched far beyond normal limits or capacity or ability to handle; strained. Page 113.

over-the-counter: directly to a customer, without requiring a doctor's prescription. Page 7.

P

palliative: treating symptoms only, without eliminating the cause. Page 56.

Palm Springs, California: a desert community in southeastern California, a state on the west coast of the United States. Page 97.

Pantelleria: a Mediterranean island strategically located between the island of Sicily and the coast of North Africa. A part of Italy, Pantelleria was heavily fortified during World War II (1939–1945) and, in the spring of 1943, was the target of heavy bombing by Allied forces. Pantelleria surrendered on 11 June 1943, opening the door to the subsequent invasion of Sicily by Allied forces. Page 38.

paradin': a spelling that represents an informal pronunciation of the word *parading,* walking around so as to show or display (something) proudly, as if in a formal parade. Page 116.

parka: a large, windproof, hooded jacket for use in cold weather. Page 29.

Parsimony, Principle of: a logical principle according to which no more causes or forces should be assumed than are necessary to account for the facts. *Parsimony* means extreme or excessive management of resources so that nothing is wasted. Page 25.

party: a person or group that participates in some action, affair, plan, etc. Page 27.

party line: the authorized or agreed-upon policies and practices of a group, or the ideas and aims of its leaders. Page 106.

passin' off: a spelling that represents an informal pronunciation of *passing off,* misrepresenting as something else; offering (something) under false pretenses or with the intent to deceive. Page 117.

patently: obviously, plainly or clearly. Page 76.

Pathfinder: a weekly magazine that covered American politics, international news, literary and movie reviews and fiction, published in Washington, DC. Page 41.

PC bridge: *PC* is an abbreviation for *patrol coastal,* a class of fast naval patrol vessels, also referred to as *submarine chasers.* During World War II (1939–1945), one of the naval vessels that L. Ron Hubbard served on was the *PC-815,* which he commanded in patrols off the Pacific Northwest coast. (A *bridge* is an elevated platform built above the upper deck of a vessel and from which a ship is navigated.) Page 54.

peddled: promoted as an idea or belief continuously. Page 59.

Pekingese: a small pet dog of a Chinese breed with a short, flat nose, a long, straight, silky coat and a tail that curls over its back. Page 54.

penicillin: a drug that kills bacteria and is used to treat a wide range of infections. Page 7.

penned: wrote with, or as if with, a pen. Page 98.

peptic ulcer: a sore formed on the lining of the stomach or adjacent organs due to secretion of excess digestive acid, sometimes causing chronic stomach pain. *Peptic* means pertaining to or associated with digestion. Page 20.

perceptic: any sense message such as a sight, sound, smell, etc. Page 28.

perforce: unavoidably or as forced by circumstances. Page 105.

pervasive: spreading through or into every part of; widespread. Page 50.

P-400: a version of the P-39 that was originally planned for use by other Allied countries but was also used by the US. The two planes were virtually identical, differing mainly in the type of aircraft guns used. *See also* **P-39.** Page 38.

Ph. D.: an abbreviation for *Doctor of Philosophy,* the highest level of university degree that can be attained, awarded to someone who has successfully completed a lengthy piece of original research. Page 39.

phenobarbital: a white, odorless powder used as a sedative or sleeping pill. Page 66.

Phoenix: capital and largest city in Arizona, a state in the southwestern United States. Page 114.

'phone: short for *telephone.* Page 65.

photo litho: a copy made by *photolithography,* the procedure of printing from a plate that has been prepared by photographing the image to be printed onto the plate, then treating the nonprinting area so that it repels ink, allowing only the image to be printed to take up ink. Page 92.

physical medicine: the branch of medicine concerned with the diagnosis of injuries or physical conditions and their treatment by external means, including heat, massage or exercise, rather than by medication or surgery. Page 71.

physical sciences: any of the sciences, such as physics and chemistry, that study and analyze the nature and properties of energy and nonliving matter. Page 49.

physical tone: condition or state of the body, especially as manifested by the natural firmness of muscles or of the body generally. Page 74.

ping-pong match: a condition or situation likened to a game of ping-pong (table tennis), in which an issue or subject bounces back and forth rapidly and regularly between individuals. Page 106.

pinned down: held firmly so as to restrict or prevent motion or change; bound or held to a course of action without choice. Page 90.

pitched: thrown with great force or vigor. Page 43.

pitfall(s): a hidden or unexpected disaster or difficulty. From the literal idea of a *pitfall,* a trap that is a deep hole in the ground (pit) disguised with leaves covering its top opening and having sides so steep that escape is impossible. Page 80.

plateau: a point or stage reached after a period of development or progress. Page 17.

plaudits: enthusiastic expressions of approval. Page 54.

plot: the plan or main story of a literary or dramatic work, as a play, novel or short story. Page 22.

plumbing: reaching the bottom of; examining closely or deeply to discover or understand. Page 1.

plumb the depths: fully explore or experience the deepest or lowest part of something. Page 38.

plunged: brought or forced suddenly into an unpleasant or undesirable situation. Page 113.

p.o.: an abbreviation for *post office.* Page 17.

point of, in: as regards; in reference to. Page 31.

polio: short for *poliomyelitis,* a disease, widespread in the 1950s, that usually occurred in children and young adults. It affected the brain and spinal cord, with the symptoms ranging from fever, headache and vomiting, to very stiff and weak muscles, and sometimes left patients paralyzed (loss of voluntary movement) for life. Page 62.

Political Dianetics: a branch of Dianetics that embraces the field of group activity and organization to establish the optimum conditions and processes of leadership and intergroup relations. Page 39.

political science: the study of political organizations and institutions, especially governments. Page 76.

pondering: considering something deeply and thoroughly. Page 57.

pop psychologist: a person practicing *pop (for popular) psychology*, a type of psychology that is simplistic and that is disseminated on a commercial basis. Counseling, concepts, terms, etc., are often used superficially and popularized by certain personalities, magazines, television, newspaper columns and the like. Page 106.

portal(s): a doorway or gateway that is large or elaborate in construction; the entrance, with the immediately surrounding parts of a building, church, etc. Hence poetically, a door or gate; a means of entrance. Page 57.

Port Lyautey: a city and port in northwestern Morocco, now called Kenitra. Founded in 1912, when the French took over control of part of Morocco, the city was called Port Lyautey from 1932 to 1956. It was the site of a US naval air station until 1963. Page 38.

positive suggestion(s): also, *posthypnotic suggestion*. In hypnosis, a suggestion or command that is given to a hypnotized subject who then obeys it unknowingly. Also, any phrase or command in the mind acting like one given to a hypnotized person. Page 19.

post-traumatic epilepsy: a form of epilepsy following or resulting from trauma (physical injury). *Epilepsy* is a disorder of the nervous system that briefly interrupts the normal electrical activity of the brain, resulting in seizures and characterized by a variety of symptoms, including uncontrolled movements of the body, disorientation or confusion, sudden fear or loss of consciousness. Page 66.

postulates: things that are suggested or assumed to be true as a basis for reasoning. Page 71.

power: a state or nation having international authority or influence. Page 80.

precipitancy: excessive and unwise haste in action, without taking careful thought. Page 80.

precipitation: sudden and hurried action; sudden or unwise haste. Page 81.

preclear: from *pre-Clear*, a person not yet Clear; generally a person being audited, who is thus on the road to *Clear*, the name of a state achieved through auditing or an individual who has achieved this state. The Clear is an unaberrated person. He is rational in that he forms the best possible solutions he can on the data he has and from his viewpoint. Page 71.

preconception(s): an idea or opinion formed in advance, especially based on little or no information or experience and reflecting personal prejudices. Page 45.

predictepated: a humorous form of *predicted*, stated that (a specified event) would happen in the future. Page 118.

predispose: make inclined to do, experience, act, etc.; make subject to something. Page 44.

prefatory: serving to introduce something else, such as a main body of text. Page 26.

prefrontal lobotomy: a psychiatric operation carried out by boring holes into the skull, entering the brain and severing the nerve pathways in the two frontal lobes, resulting in the patient becoming an emotional vegetable. Page 25.

premise(s): something presumed to be true and used as a basis for developing an idea. Page 19.

prenatal: occurring, existing or taking place before birth. In Dianetics it denotes experience and incidents that take place and are recorded in the mind while in the womb prior to birth. Page 66.

preponderance: a large number or the majority. Page 39.

present time: now; the current time or moment. Page 22.

prestige: standing or estimation in the eyes of others; influence; reputation. Page 43.

presumptuous: too bold or forward; taking too much for granted. Page 69.

processing: same as *auditing,* the application of Dianetics techniques (called *processes*). Processes are directly concerned with increasing the ability of the individual to survive, with increasing his sanity or ability to reason, his physical ability and his general enjoyment of life. Page 7.

process, served a: delivered or presented a legal order (process) to appear in a court of law. Page 116.

prof: an abbreviation for *professional.* Page 85.

Professional (Auditor's) Course: a one-month, full-time course training an individual to be a professional Dianetics auditor. The course included observation and practice auditing, daily lectures and coaching. Page 84.

professionalization: the act or process of establishing as a *profession,* a paid occupation, especially one involving training and a formal qualification. Page 39.

profound: deep-reaching; very great. Page 63.

progeny: children or descendants considered as a group. Page 28.

promulgate: make something widely known. Page 80.

pronouns: words used in place of nouns. From the Latin *pro,* instead of, in the place of, plus *noun.* Examples are *he, she, it, his, hers, theirs, who, that.* Page 80.

-proof: resistant to or unaffected by. Page 30.

proofs: printed pages made as a test and used for reviewing and making corrections before final printing. Page 53.

protégé: a person under the protection or care of another, especially of a person of superior position or influence. Page 63.

province: the sphere or field of activity; the range of function. Page 28.

provision: a clause in a law, contract, agreement, etc., stating that a certain requirement must be filled or a certain condition must be met. Page 119.

provisional: arranged or existing for the present, possibly to be changed later. Page 39.

psyche: the mind. Page 63.

psychometry: testing of individuals to find out their intelligence, aptitude and various personality traits. Page 97.

psycho-neurosis: in psychiatry, a disorder in which feelings of anxiety, obsessional thoughts, compulsive acts and physical complaints without objective evidence of disease, in various degrees and patterns, dominate the personality. Page 63.

psychosomatic: *psycho* refers to mind and *somatic* refers to body; the term *psychosomatic* means the mind making the body ill or illnesses which have been created physically within the body by the mind. A description of the cause and source of psychosomatic ills is contained in *Dianetics: The Modern Science of Mental Health.* Page 1.

psychosurgery: use of brain surgery as a supposed treatment of mental disorders. Page 105.

P-39: the P-39 Airacobra, manufactured by Bell Aircraft, was one of the principal American fighter aircraft in service at the start of World War II (1939–1945). A single-seat, single-engine aircraft, the P-39 performed best at lower altitudes. More than 9,500 P-39s were built before production ended in August 1944. Page 38.

Publishers Weekly: an international newsmagazine for the book publishing and bookselling industry, founded in the United States in 1872. It provides comprehensive news on the publishing industry, with data on bestsellers, statistics and annual reviews of several thousand books. It is subscribed to by bookstores, libraries, media, literary agents, publishers and others. Page 51.

pulse dropped to normal: *pulse* is the number of times the heart beats per minute. During each heartbeat, the muscles of the heart contract, pushing blood out of the heart and into the circulatory system. *"Pulse dropped to normal"* means that the pulse rate came into a normal range for an adult of average health and fitness, usually about 70 to 75 heartbeats per minute. A pulse rate of 98 to 100 indicates that the heart is weak and cannot pump enough blood with each beat, so has to beat faster to get blood out to the rest of the body. Page 74.

punctuating: occurring or appearing at regular intervals throughout. Page 49.

punitive: inflicting, concerned with or directed toward punishment. Page 106.

purty: a spelling that represents an informal pronunciation of the word *pretty,* here meaning quite or very. Page 117.

put it (that): make a statement (that). Page 95.

Q

quackery: the practice or methods of a *quack,* a person who pretends, professionally or publicly, to skill, knowledge or qualifications he or she does not possess. Page 105.

quinine: a powerful drug with a bitter taste. Primarily used for relief of pain and fevers, quinine was once the only treatment available for malaria. However, due to its disturbing side effects, it has largely been replaced by other drugs. Page 42.

R

racial: concerning all Mankind; the human race. Page 69.

radioactive: used to describe a substance that sends out harmful energy in the form of streams of very small particles due to the decay (breaking down) of atoms within the substance. Used figuratively. Page 63.

Raines, George N.: George Neely Raines (1908–1959), a US Navy medical doctor who was chief of neuropsychiatry (a field that deals with disorders of the mind and nervous system) at the Naval Medical Center in Bethesda, Maryland. Raines was the chief psychiatrist in charge of James Forrestal, former US secretary of defense, who committed suicide during psychiatric treatment at the Bethesda Naval Medical Center. *See also* **Forrestal**. Page 105.

ransacked: searched thoroughly or vigorously, looking for something in a quick and careless way. Page 116.

rapt: involved in, fascinated by or concentrating on something to the exclusion of everything else. Page 89.

rationale: the quality or state of being *rational,* capable of using reason and good judgment. Page 28.

rattled: upset, worried or nervous; confused. Page 116.

reactive mind: that portion of the mind which files and retains physical pain and painful emotion and seeks to direct the organism solely on a stimulus-response basis. It thinks only in identities. Page 29.

realized: made real; given reality to. Page 26.

rebuff: an abrupt, blunt refusal, as of offered advice or help. Page 15.

reception: the action or fact of receiving something. Page 29.

recount: give a description of an event or experience. Page 15.

reduction: the action of taking all the charge or pain out of an incident. *Reduce* means, technically, render free of aberrative material as far as possible to make the case progress. Page 97.

refresher course(s): a course of instruction designed to bring somebody's knowledge and skills up-to-date. Page 39.

reign: have control, rule or influence; predominate or be prevalent. Page 90.

Release: in Dianetics, a Release is an individual from whom major stress and anxiety have been removed by Dianetics therapy. Page 44.

render: cause to become; make. Page 25.

repertoire: the stock of skills or techniques used in a particular field or activity. Page 82.

report: reputation or repute. Page 41.

repressions: the actions, processes or results of suppressing into the unconscious or keeping out of the conscious mind unacceptable memories or desires. Page 99.

restimulated: having had some past incident reactivated through an approximation of its content perceived in the environment of the individual. Page 20.

résumé: a summing up, a condensed statement; a summary. Page 19.

retain(ed): hire (a professional) or arrange in advance for the services of, by paying a specified fee to reserve the service. Page 118.

retelling: telling something (such as a story) again, especially in a different form or to somebody who has not heard it. Page 105.

retention: the act of continuing to hold or keep. Page 29.

reverie: a light state of "concentration" not to be confused with hypnosis; in reverie the person is fully aware of what is taking place in the present. Page 30.

ride: an exciting adventure or journey. Used figuratively. Page 63.

rights: a just and legal claim to own, hold, use or derive an advantage from creative works, property or objects or to transfer such benefits to someone else or donate them, as the owner desires. Page 79.

rivaled: equaled or matched. Page 26.

Rogers, Don (Donald): former staff member of the first Dianetics Foundation in Elizabeth, New Jersey, USA. Page 85.

rolling (something) back: cutting back or reducing (something). Page 18.

Roundtable: the name of a Dianetics discussion group during 1950. A *roundtable* is a number of persons gathered together for conference, discussion of some subject, etc., and often seated at a round table. Page 86.

royalties: payments to an author, composer or inventor consisting of a percentage of the income from the individual's book, piece of music or invention. Page 82.

rugged: tough or difficult; requiring much effort, strength or endurance. Page 63.

run: audited or processed. Page 67.

run up against: suddenly be faced with an unexpected problem; hit into. Page 57.

S

sacred: not to be challenged or disrespected; regarded with deep respect, as if associated with divine things. Page 57.

salutary: of value or benefit to someone or something. Page 28.

salutation: the form of words that open a letter; for example, *Dear Sir* or *Dear (person's name),* expressing the writer's greeting to the person addressed. Page 69.

salvoed: of bombs, released all at one time, as from an airplane. Page 38.

sanitarium(s): an institution for the mentally ill. Page 85.

Santa Monica: a city in southwestern California, on the Pacific Ocean; a suburb of Los Angeles. Page 106.

Satevepost: *Saturday Evening Post,* a general magazine featuring text and photographs on a wide range of subjects. The magazine was published weekly from 1821 to 1969. It went out of business in 1969 but was revived as a monthly publication in 1971. Page 51.

Savannah: a seaport on the Atlantic coast in Georgia, a southeastern state of the United States. Page 15.

scant: barely sufficient or adequate. Page 108.

scathing: bitterly severe. Page 43.

scheme: 1. a plan or a program of action. Page 8.
2. a crafty, unethical plan of action devised to cause damage or harm and to attain some end. Page 114.

Sci Am: an abbreviation for *Scientific American. See also* **Scientific American.** Page 54.

Science Is a Sacred Cow: a book written in 1950 by British-born American chemist and author Anthony Standen (1906–1993) that covers how science is revered by the ordinary man due to a lack of understanding the subject itself. The author cites numerous examples of idiotic thinking from all the sciences, the physical as well as the social sciences, including criticizing psychology for never saying anything really important about Man. (*Sacred cow* is said disapprovingly of a custom, system, etc., that has existed for a long time and that is thought to be above question or criticism. From the traditional Hindu religious belief that cows are holy.) Page 43.

Scientific American: a popular science magazine, first published in 1845. It reports on major discoveries in science and technology, especially by publishing articles written by those doing the work described. Page 51.

scientific method: a means of acquiring knowledge that employs scientific research in which a situation or problem is identified, relevant data and facts are repeatedly gathered and an answer is formulated and verified against many observations and experiments. Page 24.

Scientology: Scientology is the study and handling of the spirit in relationship to itself, universes and other life. The term Scientology is taken from the Latin *scio,* which means "knowing in the fullest sense of the word," and the Greek word *logos,* meaning "study of." In itself the word means literally "knowing how to know." Page 96.

scotched: decisively ended or stopped. Page 17.

Seattle: a city in west central Washington State in the northwestern US and a major seaport and commercial center. Page 95.

second-rater(s): someone or something of second or inferior quality or value or that lacks excellence. Page 44.

sedation: the use of drugs (called *sedatives* or *tranquilizers*) to induce sleep or reduce nervous tension. Large doses of such drugs can create a hypnotic effect. Sedatives are habit-forming and can cause severe addiction problems. Page 105.

Seine: a river in France, flowing northwest through Paris to the English Channel, 480 miles (773 kilometers) long. Page 7.

semantics, general: a philosophical approach to language, developed by Alfred Korzybski (1879–1950), which sought a scientific basis for a clear understanding of the difference between words and reality and the ways in which words themselves can influence and limit Man's ability to think. Korzybski believed that men unthinkingly identify words with the objects they represent and have nonoptimum reactions to words based on past experiences. He also developed a highly organized system of the different categories of perceptions (called sensations) and created a precise table displaying their various physical characteristics and properties. Page 29.

semi: partially or somewhat. Page 61.

seminal: highly influential in the development of future events. Page 97.

sentiment: one's feelings with regard to something; mental attitudes (of approval or disapproval, etc.); opinions or views as to what is right or agreeable. Page 81.

served a process: delivered or presented a legal order (process) to appear in a court of law. Page 113.

set the stage: prepare the way for or provide the underlying basis or background for something. Literally, used in the theater for the action of arranging actors and objects on the stage prior to the beginning of a play or an act in a play. Page 26.

7/11: referring to the date, July 11. Page 86.

seven key, number: an analogy made by LRH between the reactive mind and an adding machine in which the number seven key has been held down so that it is always added into every computation. Of course it cannot compute correctly or get correct answers from data as long as this condition exists. Page 57.

Shakespeare: William Shakespeare (1564–1616), English poet and dramatist; the most widely known author in all English literature. Page 44.

shamanism: the doctrine or system of beliefs of the *shamans,* priests or priestesses who are said to act as intermediaries between natural and supernatural worlds and to use magic to cure ailments, foretell the future and contact and control spiritual forces. Page 31.

sharpies: very alert people. Page 52.

sheer: considered by itself without reference to anything else. Page 34.

shell: a metal container filled with explosives that can be fired from a large gun over long distances. Page 38.

side chair: a straight-backed wooden chair. Page 114.

sidestepped: evaded or avoided as if by physical movement. Page 106.

signed column: a column written with the name of the writer included. A *column* is an item in a newspaper or magazine that is always written by the same person or is always about the same subject. *Signed* means having one's name on something. Page 56.

sinking: (of a state or condition) becoming worse and worse; deteriorating. Page 81.

sinusitis: inflammation of a sinus or the sinuses (the spaces in the bones behind a person's nose). Page 20.

sketchy: giving only the main points, with little detail. Page 41.

skillion: an enormous or inconceivably large number. An intensification of *million*. Page 49.

skunk cabbage: a plant of the swampy areas of North America, known for its unpleasant, skunklike odor. The leaves of the skunk cabbage are broad and 1 to 3 feet (30 to 91 centimeters) long. Page 22.

slot, letter: a long, narrow opening in a door or in a wall near the entrance of a building, through which letters, etc., are delivered. Page 117.

slotted: placed or positioned, as in a sequence or series; included. Page 49.

slow-drawl: marked by speaking in a slow manner and drawing out certain sounds, characteristic of the Southern states of the US. Used figuratively. Page 49.

slush fund: a sum of money used for dishonest or illegal activities in politics or business, including bribery. Page 114.

snoose: a type of moist, powdered tobacco that is placed against the gums for an extended period, particularly used in Scandinavian countries. Page 51.

snuff: a preparation of tobacco, either powdered and taken into the nostrils by inhalation, or ground and placed between the cheek and gum. Page 51.

sociopolitical: of, about or signifying the combination or interaction of social and political factors. Page 106.

somatic: the word *somatic* is used in Dianetics to denote physical pain or discomfort of any kind. It can mean actual pain, such as that caused by a cut or a blow; or it can mean discomfort, as from heat or cold; it can mean itching—in short, anything physically uncomfortable. It is a non-survival physical state of being. Page 30.

sonic: recalling a sound by hearing it again. Page 31.

so to speak: one could say; to use a manner of speaking; figuratively speaking. Page 44.

Southern Pacific Railroad: a major railroad company founded in the late 1800s and responsible for construction of thousands of miles of rail lines throughout the southwestern and western parts of the United States. Page 117.

Spencer: Herbert Spencer (1820–1903), English philosopher known for his application of the scientific doctrines of evolution to philosophy and ethics. He argued that evolution, the principles of which originally came from early Indian (Eastern) writings, is actually a progressive movement where individual beings change their characteristics and habits until they are perfectly adapted to circumstances and no more change is called for. Page 99.

sperm sequence: the sequence of incidents that happen to the sperm before conception and which can contain pain and unconsciousness. Page 85.

Spinoza: Benedict (Baruch) Spinoza (1632–1677), Dutch philosopher who believed that "God, or Nature" was the only substance and all that existed. He believed that God and Nature are the same thing; that all objects and thought are forms or manifestations of God. Page 52.

Spitfire: a single-seat British fighter aircraft that was one of the fastest and most effective fighters of World War II (1939–1945). Known for its maneuverability, good climbing rate and speed, it was also heavily armed with machine guns and bombs. Page 38.

spreading their palms: a reference to the action of a priest getting ready to administer the last rites to a sick or dying person. In the Catholic Church, the priest lays his hands on the sick or dying person and prays. Page 51.

spurt: gush or flow out rapidly and in large quantities. Page 38.

squalor: shabbiness and filth resulting from poverty or neglect. Page 8.

staff physician(s): a physician who practices medicine in a clinic or hospital and commonly supervises trainees as a significant part of his work. A staff physician has final responsibility, legally and otherwise, for patient care, even when many of the minute-to-minute decisions are being made by subordinate medical staff. In the United States, staff physicians are also called *attending physicians*. Page 72.

stage, set the: prepare the way for or provide the underlying basis or background for something. Literally, used in the theater for the action of arranging actors and objects on the stage prior to the beginning of a play or an act in a play. Page 26.

staggers: moves unsteadily, as if under a great weight. Page 82.

stagnation: the state or condition of being stopped in development, growth, progress or advance. Page 81.

stake in, a: something to gain or lose; an interest in. Page 43.

stand: a position or attitude regarding a particular subject. Page 81.

stepping-stone: a stage or step that helps achieve a goal. Page 81.

stifle: prevent the development of something; inhibit; restrain. Page 96.

still devastated Japan: a reference to the state of Japan in 1950. At the end of World War II (1939–1945), one-quarter of its buildings lay in ashes due to repeated bombings of cities and atomic bombs dropped on the cities of Hiroshima and Nagasaki. Production was only one-third of its prewar level and it was not until 1955 that Japan's economy returned to its prewar levels. Page 78.

stop order: a notice made by a depositor to his bank, directing the bank to refuse payment on a specific check drawn by the depositor. Page 117.

storm, take (took) by: create a great impression upon; captivate; become quickly popular or famous. Page 1.

St. Petersburg: a city in western Florida (a southeastern state in the United States), near Tampa. Page 74.

straightwire: apply *Straightwire,* an auditing process consisting of stringing a line between present time and some incident in the past and stringing that line directly and without any detours. This enables the preclear to locate the source of the difficulty, an engram that has a command value over him. By seeing that there is a difference of time and space in the condition then and the condition now, the preclear can bring the condition under his own control. Page 95.

straits: a position of difficulty, distress or need. Page 114.

Street & Smith: a large American publishing company established in the mid-1800s that put out a large number of periodicals and pulp magazines in the late nineteenth and early twentieth centuries, such as *Astounding Science Fiction* magazine and *Unknown* magazine. Page 35.

stress analysis: the determination of the stresses produced in a solid body, such as a bridge or a building, when subjected to various forces, such as weight, wind, earthquake, gravity, etc. Used figuratively by LRH in reference to reviewing the results of the improvements in people he was treating. Page 17.

sturdily: in a manner characterized by firmness and determination; unwaveringly. Page 80.

subatomic: of or relating to the phenomena occurring inside of atoms or particles smaller than atoms. Page 34.

subsidize: support something by grants of money. Page 89.

subsidy: a grant or contribution of money; monetary assistance granted by a government to a person or group in support of an enterprise regarded as being in the public interest; financial assistance given by one person or government to another. Page 90.

succinct: briefly and clearly expressed. Page 50.

sulfa: a group of drugs (sulfa drugs) that aid in treating infections, burns and the like by preventing the further growth of bacteria. Page 8.

sullen: showing silent resentment; angry and silent. Page 31.

summation: a review of previously stated facts or statements, often with a final conclusion or conclusions drawn from them. Page 101.

Sunday, all ways for: a variation of *forty (or six) ways to Sunday,* meaning in every way possible, in a comprehensive fashion. Page 117.

sun, under the: in the world; on Earth. Page 72.

Superior court: a court in some states of the United States that can hear and decide any civil or criminal case. Originally, such courts were established at a level above lower courts that heard and decided only certain types of cases. Page 116.

superman: someone like *Superman,* a comic strip character created in 1938. *Superman* is an almost invincible (incapable of being defeated or beaten because of great strength or skill) crime-fighting superhero. Page 17.

supplanted: replaced by something else. Page 100.

surmised: concluded or supposed that something was possible or likely. Page 80.

sweeping: wide in range or effect. Page 100.

syndication: publication simultaneously, or supplying for simultaneous publication, in a number of newspapers or other periodicals in different places. Page 56.

T
_____

taciturn: habitually uncommunicative or reserved in speech and manner. Page 34.

tactile: the sense of touch. Page 28.

take stock: think carefully about something so as to form an opinion about it or determine what one will do. Page 57.

Tampa 6, Florida: a seaport and tourist resort in Florida, a state in the southeastern United States. The *6* was a designation for the postal district the letter was to be sent to. Page 73.

taste: 1. a first experience or a sample of something. Page 53.
2. a tendency to like or enjoy a particular thing or type of thing. Page 81.

telling: revealing; indicative of much otherwise unnoticed; that tells or reveals much. Page 16.

tended: cared for or looked after. Page 29.

tenement: a run-down and often overcrowded apartment house, especially in a poor section of a large city. Page 8.

tenets: principles, doctrines. Page 42.

ten quart creek: a humorous reference to a small stream (creek) containing only 10 quarts of water (2.5 gallons or 9.5 liters). Page 54.

terms: 1. particular words or combinations of words, especially those used to mean something very specific or used in a specialized area of knowledge or work. Page 58.

2. the particular requirements laid down formally in an agreement or contract. Page 61.

Terra Incognita: an unknown or unexplored land, region or subject. The term is Latin for "unknown land." Page 2.

thanks a million: an informal expression of deep gratitude or great appreciation. Page 11.

Thanksgiving: Thanksgiving Day, celebrated in the United States on the fourth Thursday of November, to remember the feast held in 1621 by the colonists from England who had set up a settlement at Plymouth, in what is now southeastern Massachusetts. Native Americans had shown the colonists how to grow food and the feast gave thanks to God for plentiful crops and good health. The customary turkey dinner now served at Thanksgiving is a reminder of the wild turkeys served at that first Thanksgiving celebration. Page 7.

thiotimoline: a made-up name for a chemical compound conceived by science fiction author Isaac Asimov (1920–1992). Thiotimoline first appeared in a 1948 Asimov story that made fun of typical scientific research papers. Page 36.

this here: used to emphasize what follows. Page 17.

three-thousand-cycle note: a high-pitched sound. *Cycle* refers to a vibration. The more vibrations a sound wave has, the higher the pitch. Page 42.

Time: an American weekly magazine first published in 1923 in New York City, New York, USA. Page 41.

Times: a reference to the *New York Times*. *See also* **New York Times.** Page 54.

time track: the timespan of the individual from conception to present time on which lies the sequence of events of his life. Page 44.

Tomorrow: a magazine that focused on topics in mysticism and *parapsychology,* the study of mental phenomena, such as hypnosis, telepathy, etc., that are not understood by more traditional scientific fields. *Tomorrow* was published between 1942 and 1962. Page 54.

tone: 1. the physical state or condition of something, as of the body or an organ. Page 74.

2. a particular mental state or disposition; spirit, character or mood. Page 89.

Tone Scale: in Dianetics, a scale by which a state of mind can be graded. It is divided in the following bands, ranging from the highest to the lowest: Tone band 4 is where the person is happy mentally, 3 is a zone of general happiness and well-being, 2 is a level of bearable existence, 1 is anger, 0 is apathy. Page 74.

took root: became fixed or established. Page 70.

Topeka: a city in the northeast part of Kansas, a state in the central United States, and location of the Menninger Clinic, a mental health facility founded by the Menninger family of American psychiatrists. Page 106.

t'other: an older way of spelling *the other*. Page 17.

to wit: used to introduce a list or explanation of what one has just mentioned. Originally a phrase used in law, *that is to wit,* which meant that is to know, that is to say. Page 49.

tractable: easily managed or controlled. Page 25.

trademarks: symbols, designs, words, letters, etc., that are used to distinguish a product of an organization, legally registered and protected by law. Page 114.

trance: a half-conscious state, seemingly between sleeping and waking. Page 19.

trauma: emotional shock following a stressful event. Page 2.

treatise: a formal, usually extensive, written work on a subject. Page 72.

try out: use experimentally; test. Page 79.

turn loose: make free; release. Page 117.

twin-engine aircraft: an airplane powered by two engines. Page 106.

U

umbilical cord: a long narrow tube of flesh that joins an unborn baby to its mother. Page 20.

unassailable: not subject to denial or dispute. Page 69.

unbalanced: unable to make sound judgments. Page 27.

uncordial: unfriendly; not warm or courteous. Page 85.

undermine: weaken or cause to collapse by removing underlying support, as by digging away or eroding the foundation. Used figuratively. Page 106.

unfounded: not supported by evidence or facts. Page 108.

unleash: let loose from control or restraint, as if freeing from a leash; suddenly release. Page 1.

unprecedented: new; not done before. Page 113.

unsullied: (of the purity, perfection or luster of something) not marred or corrupted; unstained. Page 81.

untoward: unfavorable or unfortunate. Page 21.

untrammeled: not limited or restricted, as by regulations; open or accessible. Page 26.

unwarranted: not justified or deserved. Page 108.

up and: an informal phrase used to show that something was done suddenly and abruptly. Page 116.

uprooted: picked up all of one's belongings and moved from a place where one has lived for a long time to another location or area. Page 113.

uvea: the middle of the three layers that make up the eyeball that includes the iris (colored part of the eye), muscles and tissues surrounding the lens of the eye. Page 74.

uveitis: inflammation of the *uvea*. *See also* **uvea**. Page 73.

V

validation: official confirmation or approval of a procedure or activity. Page 92.

Van: a nickname of Alfred Elton van Vogt (1912–2000), Canadian-born science fiction writer who began his decades-long career during science fiction's Golden Age (1939–1949). Esteemed in the science fiction field, van Vogt was presented the Grand Master Award by the Science Fiction Writers of America in 1995. Page 85.

Vedic: pertaining to the *Veda* or *Vedic Hymns,* the earliest recorded philosophic writings. They are the most ancient sacred literature of the Hindus, comprising over a hundred books still in existence. They tell about evolution, about Man coming into this universe and the curve of life, which is birth, growth, degeneration and decay. The word *veda* means knowledge. Page 99.

vehicle: a medium of communication, expression or display. Page 34.

venture: an undertaking; something embarked upon. Page 82.

Verne, Jules: (1828–1905) French novelist and the first great specialist of science fiction. He anticipated flights into outer space, submarines, helicopters, air conditioning, guided missiles and motion pictures long before they were developed. Page 58.

vestigial: forming a very small remnant of something that was once larger, as in size or scope. Page 64.

virtue: the worth, advantage or beneficial quality of something. Page 32.

V-2: a powerful German missile of World War II (1939–1945), the first rocket to surpass the speed of sound and the forerunner of modern rockets. Page 41.

W

wafting: floating gently through the air. Page 49.

wake of, in the: *wake* is the visible trail (of agitated and disturbed water) left by something, such as a ship, moving through water. Hence a condition left behind someone or something that has passed; following as a consequence. Page 62.

war lords: military leaders, especially of a warlike nation. Page 81.

warn't: a spelling that represents an informal pronunciation of *was not*. Page 117.

warped: literally, bent or twisted out of shape, especially out of a straight or flat form. Figuratively, *warped* means twisted or distorted from the truth, fact, true meaning, etc. Page 107.

warrant(s): a document that gives police particular rights or powers—for example, the right to search or arrest somebody. Page 118.

West Coast: the western coast of the United States, bordering the Pacific Ocean and comprising the coastal areas of California, Oregon and Washington. Page 72.

West Douglas Avenue: a street in *Wichita,* a city in south central Kansas (a state in the central US), the home of the Hubbard Dianetic Research Foundation in 1951 and early 1952. Page 113.

Western Union: a major American telegraph company founded in 1856. *Telegraph* is a method of long-distance communication originally conveying messages as coded electric impulses transmitted through wires, now conveyed by radio, satellites and other modern means of transmission. Page 92.

whar: a spelling that represents an informal pronunciation of the word *where.* Page 117.

whipped up: made or prepared very quickly. Page 54.

Wichita: a city in Kansas (a state in the central US) and the location of a Hubbard Dianetic Research Foundation in 1951 and 1952. Page 3.

wild-eyed: extremely enthusiastic and determined. Page 50.

wildfire, like: with great speed, from the fact that *wildfire,* an intense fire usually in a wilderness area, spreads rapidly. Page 82.

wild flowers, like: emerging or appearing rapidly and in volume without any effort or work. A *wild flower* is a flower of a plant that normally grows in fields, forests, etc., without deliberate planting or care. Page 50.

Winchell, Walter: (1897–1972) famous US journalist and broadcaster whose newspaper columns and radio news broadcasts gave him a massive audience and great influence in the United States in the 1930s, 1940s and 1950s. Page 49.

wind break: something that breaks the force of the wind; some structure serving as a shelter from the wind. Page 22.

Winter, Dr.: a doctor who, in the early 1950s, was involved in Dianetics. Page 85.

wised up: made aware or informed about something. Page 118.

witch of a day: a terrible day, likened to a *witch,* an ugly or mean old woman. Page 63.

works, the: everything; all related items or matters. Page 57.

wrinkles: helpful or valuable hints or tips, clever tricks or pieces of useful information, knowledge or advice. Page 85.

writ: 1. a court order authorizing the seizure of property, as to cover debts. Page 113.

2. an older form of *wrote,* the past tense of the verb *write.* Page 116.

wry: grimly humorous with a hint of bitterness. Page 114.

Y

yard goods: literally, fabrics sold by the yard (three feet or approximately one meter). *Goods* refers to articles for sale, especially fabric. Hence, in reference to Dianetics, *"showing yard goods"* means that the auditor lets a person find out about the subject for himself or herself without suggestion or evaluation. Page 43.

yardstick: any standard of measurement or judgment. Page 28.

Yoga: a school of Indian religious philosophy advocating and prescribing a course of physical and mental disciplines for attaining liberation from the material world and union of the self with a supreme spirit. Page 59.

INDEX

low reality cases, 92

Lucretius

philosophy of, 99

M

malaria, 27

Dianetics and rapid improvement
from, 31

engram and, 29

Man

unconscious experiences, liability to, 29

manic

engrams and, 29

mankind

freedom and, 81

Manney, E. E.

Wichita Publishing Company
photograph, 114

Mathieu, Hubert "Matty," 7, 8

Mayo Clinic, 71

May, Rollo

critical review of *Dianetics*, 106

medicine

Dianetics and, 28

medicine drumming, 30

memorandum

organizational, 90

Menninger Clinic, 106

mental aberration

source of, 29

mental frontiers

involvement in the complexities
of, 27

mental health monopoly

letters to, 105

mind

character of, re-definition, 18

miracles

chronic colitis handled, 51

girl walking, 1

longshoreman, 8

vision improvement, 74

Morey, Morgan J.

letter from, 73

motor strip

sensory perceptions, 30

Music Hall, Kansas City, Missouri

photograph, 92

N

natural drives

inhibited by engrams, 29

New York longshoreman

letter, 7, 10

New York (NY) Times

story on Dianetics, 49, 51

**New York State Commission against
Discrimination,** 56

number seven key, 57

O

Oak Knoll Naval Hospital

research trail
endocrinological studies, 15

Ochsner Clinic, 71

W

THE
L. RON HUBBARD
SERIES

"To really know life," L. Ron Hubbard wrote, "you've got to be part of life. You must get down and look, you must get into the nooks and crannies of existence. You have to rub elbows with all kinds and types of men before you can finally establish what he is."

Through his long and extraordinary journey to the founding of Dianetics and Scientology, Ron did just that. From his adventurous youth in a rough and tumble American West to his far-flung trek across a still mysterious Asia; from his two-decade search for the very essence of life to the triumph of Dianetics and Scientology—such are the stories recounted in the L. Ron Hubbard Biographical Publications.

Drawn from his own archival collection, this is Ron's life as he himself saw it. With each volume of the series focusing upon a separate field of endeavor, here are the compelling facts, figures, anecdotes and photographs from a life like no other.

Indeed, here is the life of a man who lived at least twenty lives in the space of one.

FOR FURTHER INFORMATION VISIT
www.lronhubbard.org

The L. Ron Hubbard Series
A PROFILE

To order copies of *The L. Ron Hubbard Series*
or L. Ron Hubbard's Dianetics and
Scientology books and lectures, contact:

US AND INTERNATIONAL

BRIDGE PUBLICATIONS, INC.
5600 E. Olympic Blvd.
Commerce, California 90022 USA
www.bridgepub.com
Tel: (323) 888-6200
Toll-free: 1-800-722-1733

UNITED KINGDOM AND EUROPE

NEW ERA PUBLICATIONS
INTERNATIONAL ApS
Smedeland 20
2600 Glostrup, Denmark
www.newerapublications.com
Tel: (45) 33 73 66 66
Toll-free: 00-800-808-8-8008